IT ONLY GETS FUNNIER

True Adventures of Bluewater Cruising

Comically Narrated by Author, John "Luke" Lucarell

Copyright © 2016 John C Lucarell.

All rights reserved. No part of this book may be reproduced, stored, or transmitted by any means—whether auditory, graphic, mechanical, or electronic—without written permission of both publisher and author, except in the case of brief excerpts used in critical articles and reviews. Unauthorized reproduction of any part of this work is illegal and is punishable by law.

ISBN: 978-1-4834-6292-9 (sc)
ISBN: 978-1-4834-6294-3 (hc)
ISBN: 978-1-4834-6293-6 (e)

Library of Congress Control Number: 2016921093

Because of the dynamic nature of the Internet, any web addresses or links contained in this book may have changed since publication and may no longer be valid. The views expressed in this work are solely those of the author and do not necessarily reflect the views of the publisher, and the publisher hereby disclaims any responsibility for them.

Any people depicted in stock imagery provided by Thinkstock are models, and such images are being used for illustrative purposes only.
Certain stock imagery © Thinkstock.

Cover image by https://www.facebook.com/TheCartoonistMe

Lulu Publishing Services rev. date: 12/28/2016

A message from the author

These pages feature excessive exclamation marks and mathematical calculations performed either by professionals or under the influence of professionals under the influence. This is a work of creative storytelling centered on actual events. I hope that you, my reader, forgive me for not paying attention in my English classes but enjoy these accounts and are inspired to take to the water yourself.

Disclaimer — I absolutely must insist that no one attempt to recreate or re-enact any stunt or any other strenuous activity that was carried out during these voyages. Some names and identifying details have been changed to protect the privacy of the people and places involved.

Contents

CHAPTER 1	The Departure	1
CHAPTER 2	My Early Bluewater Cruising	9
CHAPTER 3	Memorable Moments on the Intracoastal Waterway	17
CHAPTER 4	Memorable Moments on the St Johns River	24
CHAPTER 5	My First Distress Call	29
CHAPTER 6	Charter Fishing Trip	36
CHAPTER 7	My Three Captains!	39
CHAPTER 8	Sailing – What Was I Thinking?	43
CHAPTER 9	I'm Still Sailing - Days Later	49
CHAPTER 10	South America Delivery	54
CHAPTER 11	Cartagena, Colombia	62
CHAPTER 12	Long Day Ahead	69
CHAPTER 13	Same Day – How's that Possible?	74
CHAPTER 14	Bocas Del Toro, Panama	81
CHAPTER 15	San Andres, Colombia	87
CHAPTER 16	Weather Delay - Roatan, Honduras	91
CHAPTER 17	Roatan, Honduras to Isla Mujeres, Mexico	95
CHAPTER 18	Weather Delay - Isla Mujeres, Mexico	99
CHAPTER 19	Next Stop Home – Mexico to the USA	103

CHAPTER 1
The Departure

My most memorable Bluewater journey began back on a cold December when an old friend of mine called to see if I was up for a "bumpy ride"—a term, you must understand, that always means **boat delivery**. This friend, Captain Kevin, is also known as Captain Cub or Cubby, a name he received many years ago from another dear friend of ours, Shawn. On a few yearly trips, you would find Kevin sleeping in cubby holes on overnight excursions from Sanford, Florida, on the St. Johns River to St Augustine, Florida over on the coast.

Oh, yeah! Those two saddled me with my nickname of "VD," on that winter day when we went skiing in North Carolina. The three of us were standing on top of a very steep mountain, looking down into a perilous V-shaped drop. Yes, this was the one with the warning sign: "Caution Double Black Diamond, Expert Skiers Only!" Well, they pushed me; they did, and "VD" (Vertical Drop) stuck. I still suffer from the nightmares of hearing my own screams and their laughter and feeling the bumps and fear as I tumbled and crashed down the mountain—not to mention the x-rays and pain to follow. I still—to this day, suffer from Chionophobia. (It's in the dictionary; just Google it!)

That same ski trip, Cubby also became known as "Kid Psycho" because of his destructive skiing abilities and thundering wipeouts. For your own well-being, you just didn't get in his way. Kevin, though, had a presence: he could walk into a room, and people would take notice. You know, it was like that tall, rugged James Bond appeal. Kevin was the ultimate epitome of "Cool!" Just imagine the scenario as a lovely woman goes out on a blind date with James Bond, played by Kevin:

[Bond] I admire your courage for going out with me, Miss...?
[Woman] Fuchigami, Chiasa Fuchigami. ("Chiasa," Japanese "one thousand mornings.") I admire your luck, Mr...?
[Bond] Cub, Kevin Cub.

(Ah, nope. Okay, how about trying *Cubby, Kevin Cubby?* Nope, the name just doesn't work as well as Bond, James Bond. Sorry, Cub!)

Photograph by: John Lucarell
Captain "Cub"

And, then there's Captain Shawn, the shy, tall, long-haired handsome ladies' man, and his up-and-coming talented rock group "McAlley Lain." You know the type. On the slopes, I just called him "Hawkeye," as he flew down the hills with his long, rudder-like hair and his flapping arms: looking for prey. I remember the three of us standing on the mountain — I quickly pointed out three women about 50 yards down the slope. I was giving some advice on how to meet someone while skiing without having to say anything.

I tell Hawk, "Look. Ski down, and just before you get there fall and look like you're hurt. I promise they'll come over to help."

Well, off he goes down the mountain and into a stunt snow dive. I have seen no one wipe out intentionally like he did. It's a hard process to describe, but it's kind of like doing surgery on yourself. The move I call a "Shooter Seizure," it's like a double barrel roll with a combined backflip and a well executed 180 thrown in for good measure. After his stunt skiing performance, the girls laughed, turned and continued down the mountain. Nope, I don't think they laughed; that was Cub and I laughing as we hovered over his expressionless snow-covered—humiliated—body. I don't recall if he ever asked for my advice again! Right, he didn't ask for it this time. (Hawk will have that same vacuous look in Chapter 2.)

I remember the night when the Hawk took me to a local bar. I swear this guy never bought a drink for himself; the women came from everywhere bearing drinks and gifts and more drinks as if he were an endangered species. I counted at least five alcohol assists. Never in my life has this happened to me!

"How do you do it?" I asked.

"Dude, it's the trench coat," he answered.

"So, if I go out and buy a trench coat, that's it?"

"Sorry," he said, "I don't think that's going to work for you!"

His cold and piercing words briefly shattered my confidence. I was determined after this embarrassing setback to never lose to him at golf! (Remember, this book is based on actual events!)

Before leaving for my memorable December trip, one delivery that immediately comes to mind and still makes me laugh just thinking about it was over twenty years ago from Isla Mujeres, Mexico, to Ft.

Lauderdale, Florida. I was aboard a 92' yacht named OTHER SHORE towing a 43' sportfish, christened ANTICIPATION. On this adventure, another good friend who worked with me at the marina accompanied me. He wasn't just a friend: I often called Charles, "Scooter, My Son!" The plan was to fly into Cancun, Mexico, from Orlando, Florida, to meet up with Cub. As usual, nothing was going as planned, and we found ourselves three hours behind schedule due to several flight delays. The only instruction I had from Captain Cub when arriving in Cancun was to "take a taxi from the airport, and we'll meet you at Casa De Marina."

In route from the Cancun International Airport and about thirty minutes later, the taxi driver turns and asks, "What Casa De Marina do you want to go to?" I definitely do not want to hear that.

"Well," I ask, "how many Casa De Marinas do you have?"

"Dos."

"Okay, how about you drop us off at the "uno" we're heading to, and we'll go from there."

Did you notice that I responded with a little Spanish in that last sentence? I would've hammered this guy with at least a whole sentence in Spanish if I had bothered to pay attention in class. I enjoyed high school instead of studying back in the late 60s. I remember the day we locked the substitute Spanish teacher in the closet. I can only imagine what the principal would've said if the teacher hadn't laughed with the rest of the class—She had turned my good friend Steve and me in!

So, we finally reach hotel "uno." I tell Scoot to watch our luggage and expensive weather gear while I go around back to see if the boat is there. Oh No! There's nothing but small boats docked at this marina and Cubby shafted me again for not paying attention to his instructions! Just as I'm walking back towards Scoot to give him the bad news, I hear my name. It's Bill (Cub's first mate at the time) aboard the sportfish. He informs me that we must take the sportfish out to Isla Mujeres, an island three or so miles off the coast.

Cub never goes into detail about anything, let alone being understandable because of his soft voice. However, if you messed up, that voice throttled up, Boy! You sure could hear him then, every single word! But, with no volume adjustment to Cub's standard serene dialog,

I could usually make out about one out of five of his words. It's like playing Charades!

We arrived at Isla Mujeres around ten o'clock that evening, and the first thing we did was drink. I'm not a big drinker on any scale. (That comes later in the book.) I don't even recall if we said much of a Hello, let alone remembering the warning from friends –

"Do NOT, repeat, do NOT drink the tap water when visiting a foreign country including any of the flavored-ice cocktails" that Scooter and I were about to consume! So, it's wise to be aware of what you are drinking and eating when visiting another country. So stop blaming them as a whole for your delicate stomach.

Hey, alcohol silences common sense. Yes, I'll have another one of those well-cooked, aromatic street tacos before all of us head to a restaurant on a rooftop for dinner where Scooter will be introduced to the infamous "Montezuma's Revenge."

I'm even surprised that I remember any of this, but…… Oh Yeah – a little later we find ourselves on the beach at a packed palapa-style bar with sand floors and a combination of swings and hammocks. I was told this is a favorite hangout for visitors to this beautiful place. The restaurant and bar are part of one of the hotels at the northern end of the island.

At one point, sometime early the next morning, Scoot says, "Do you think we should leave now and try to figure out where the boat is?"

I replied in a less than clear dialog: "Cub is out on the dance floor, and as soon as he returns, I'll check."

It wasn't long before Cub was back, and, sure enough, he sounded just like me: "Me Lu bah ki peeke boo scootha miya huh?"

Before we could respond Cub was back out on the dance floor busting his legendary Cubby moves, where the body is in motion except for the feet. I taught him that!

A short time later, we decided to head back and try to locate our boat! I will always remember the three of us around four in the morning, doing the Laverne & Shirley theme song as we skipped down the dark city streets: "One, two, three; schlemiel, schlimazel, hasenpfeffer." Then – faster than my imagination could take me – we were surrounded by the Mexican Military carrying rather large weapons. I do believe they were laughing at our street rendition, and when we told them where we were trying to go, they politely escorted us safely back to the marina without firing a shot.

Next, we tried to get Cub in the boat, and he said something funny like: "Me Lu bah ki peeke boo scootha miya huh?" But, in his slurred, soft-spoken voice making it more entertaining! You would've thought by now I'd figured out what that was? I could only wonder if the military were watching with their version of Charades, trying to act out what he was trying to say?

"Oh, no," we told him. "No way are we letting you back off this boat!"

"OCRAY!" AND, then he turned and threw up all over Scooter! It gets no better than this? (Well the story gets better, but later in the book.) We finally get him to bed and, soon thereafter, I retire to my stateroom: a fitting end to my long and unforgettable travel day.

About thirty minutes later, I hear someone moving topside, so I go up to check, and there's Cub.

"Hey, guys, we got to go! A storm's brewing, and it's heading our way!"

I look at him, and I ask myself, "OCRAY... Where's the slurred speech, that "peeke boo," the vomiting, and—you know—hangover?" Nothing, it's like he never had a drink! I can't do that! Can you do that?

I get Scooter up and we prep the boats for a tow since the sportfish does not have the cruising range to make it back to the states. Cub, Scoot and I stay aboard the 92, and Bill remains on the sportfish—and, off we go. We leave that same "hasenpfeffer" morning, around six o'clock, for our much-anticipated body aching, and fun boating excursion. I just wished I didn't feel so bad. I'm sure Scooter feels the same. When it's my turn to drive, I am sooo sick! Yes, alcohol plays a major role in all of this. I am nauseated with the lingering effects of my personal attack of Montezuma's Revenge.

Captain Cub sits me in the chair when it's my turn at the helm and hands me a wastepaper bucket with the warning, "Please don't puke on the instruments!" (Now, Scooter will be mad as hell when he reads this.) Scoot, My Son very seldom leaves the head (boat toilet) but does take his turn at the wheel, and, let me tell 'ya, I see some interesting facial expressions during his watch as he quickly retreats to the head for the umpteenth time. I know the feeling, Good Buddy! Scooter is an excellent boat captain; safety-minded from the bilge to the bridge and one of the most multi-talented I've ever met. Also, he sure can make you laugh with his funny impressions. I just hope he's laughing while he reads this! If it weren't for the alcohol and food being involved, things would've been better for him, but this trip wouldn't have been as comical!

So, for the next 35 pleasurable hours, we each take our turns at the helm. At five the next afternoon, just off Key West, Bill calls on the VHF marine radio and tells me the tow rope broke. So, I throttle down and wake Cub. Now let me give you this valuable information about waking the Cub. Never, ever be within ten feet when you do. I have seen him jump up with his arms swinging, legs a-kickin', and singing Nat King Cole's "Pick Yourself Up," all at the same time—trust me! Thanks to the person who invented the expandable boat hook, he never laid a hand on me. I now know all the words to "Pick Yourself Up"!

Cub tells Scooter and me to go to the cockpit and haul the line in. This was a pair of 2-3/4" water- logged lines 300' in length heading back to the sportfish. With every pull, I thought that little monster would come through my stomach, reach up and pull my tonsils out. I looked over at Scooter and told him if I had a gun I'd shoot myself. I can't even describe what he said. I can't even find the words he used in the dictionary to verify the accuracy of my memory!

So, Bill gets the sportfish ready for the short trip to Ft. Lauderdale and backs it towards the 92, stern to stern. Cub tells Scooter to go with Bill while Cub and I take the 92. The stunning end to all this is watching as the sportfish drifts away, and there I am giving that little rapid wave goodbye with my hand held close to my body. Scooter with one hand on the flybridge ladder slowly raises the other arm showing that finger that communicates moderate-to-extreme contempt. If you include the gesture and the facial expressions, he expands his meanings to include every swear word ever written! A Kodak moment if only I were in reach of my camera!

Both boats begin our movement north to Ft. Lauderdale, and remember the tropical storm heading our way? "It's here!" The winds register over 50 knots, and we lose sight of the sportfish, having no communications all night with them. The winds really do a number on the bridge, damaging canvas and leaving no antennae standing. I swear we had a hot tub on the top deck when leaving Key West! In the calming morning, we finally see Bill and Scooter—no damage! AND, yes, Scooter never left the head all night!

Chapter 2

My Early Bluewater Cruising

[I'll try to keep every adventure in chronological order so not to confuse myself.]

I started Bluewater and river boating back in November of 1971. Many of my delivery trips involved my good friends Cub and Shawn. We met while all of us worked on several dinner boats cruising the St. Johns River from Sanford, Florida, during the 1980s. Shawn has stayed in the area and recently started his airboat business, Airrow Tours, which is doing well. Cub left several years later to seek his professional calling in operating private and chartered yachts. I will say this about our Captain, in all my years around boats, I met no one more courageous and skilled at seamanship than Kevin, our Captain Cub. I often thought about leaving as well, but instead of following in Cub's wake, I decided to stay at the marina to give Shawn 26 more years to try to beat me at golf!

For Shawn, Steve, and another great friend of ours, Bud, Monday meant Golf. It wasn't your usual golf outing on the links; it was more like going into battle. One day while Shawn was about to tee off with his back to me, I launched a rather large firecracker that found its target right between his legs. When this puppy went off, he dropped to his knees like a melted snowman. It brought back memories from our skiing trip. Also, it was like watching the movie, The Shawshank Redemption when Andy Dufresne, played by Tim Robbins was standing in the rain. In this scene, Andy was in knee-deep water and looking up to the skies with his outstretched arms. Shawn was probably mumbling something like "Luke can hold you prisoner, but revenge can set you free!" And, if you saw this classic movie, you'll remember that the scene was just after crawling through 500 yards of smelly sewer foulness. Shawn had the same smell, as though he had crawled through that noxious pipe!

It wasn't many Mondays after that day Shawn found his revenge. Weeks before I had asked Steve "If Shawn hurls one at me, let me know."

"I'll yell 'incoming' if he does," replied Steve.

I was using the bathroom out on the course when I saw something bounce off the soda machine. When I looked down, I saw what looked like a mini stick of dynamite. Shawn's timely payback found its target with laser-guided accuracy. I couldn't hear anything the rest of that day! The good news for me, if any: the soda machine for the first time in weeks started to work!

I asked Steve, "What happened with 'incoming'?"

"I didn't see him throw it," was Steve's reply. Shawn told me later that Steve lit the fuse!

I was most fortunate to be Monroe Harbour Marina's Harbor Master since 1971. For over 45 years, I have had the privilege to work with some great people and a wonderful owner. This work also allowed me to meet many boaters, and I was often tempted to use any means necessary to keep them at our marina so they couldn't leave and would continue paying. [Remember, I just *thought* about it but did none of that. That lie will be covered in my next book, "Sitting Pretty, Success Before Retirement!"]

Photograph by: John Lucarell
Monroe Harbour Marina

One wild and entertaining adventure takes me back to the Bahamas. In the spring of 1984, twelve of us chartered three Morgan sailboats. Okay, of the twelve in our party, only four knew how to sail, and those four were in the same boat. Can you say "disaster in the making!" Today, you can't just call up and reserve a sailboat to charter without proof of your sailing abilities. But this was not so back then. With no experience they let us have these beauties for seven days. [I feel another few chapters and damage assessments heading your way!]

On one of those days, we had our own little regatta going and the race was on. If I remember right, Captain Brian won the race. I came in second and, yep, the actual sailors came in dead last! They didn't know we both had our engines running as well; Brian started his just before I did. The gloating began, and we poured it on. See, powerboaters and sailors just don't get along, Never! So, I've been told!

The race ended at Green Turtle Cay, and our stay here was memorable. We anchored off New Plymouth, the main settlement on Green Turtle. We decided that this was the day to do something different. Why not embarrass the whole gang! We motored our three dinghies to town and pulled up to the beach area. "Tide?" you ask. "What tide?" We all grabbed the boats and pulled them up on the beach.

"Hey, do you think we should pull the boats up some more, so they don't float away if the tide comes in?" We do, and the results come much later.

I have been in the Abacos a few times now. It is a must to visit Miss Emily's Blue Bee Bar. Back in the early 70s, this place was a small one-room building and frequently-visiting boaters often placed notes, clothing, or business cards on the walls. Luckily, I was one of the first to leave my business card on the wall to the left as you walk in; however, with the passing years you can barely make it out. My favorite drink is Miss Emily's Blue Bee Special, and if you like rum then this is the drink for you! And, if you like rum and memories? Sorry! You won't remember anything, but your friends will!

Well, the group of twelve-less-one head out to view the town. Where's the less one, you ask? That would be Brian, now Manager at Monroe Harbour Marina, sitting on a boulder outside the cemetery with Miss Emily's son who's about seven feet tall. (You see, alcohol makes everyone around you look taller, and Brian swears he doesn't remember any of this.) So, there he was, his arm around him, slurred speech and speaking in a familiar form of English, but we can't be certain: "Me Lu bah ki peeke boo scootha miya huh?" What The? Not again!

"Hey, why don't you just stay here at the cemetery because in the morning you will wish you were here, and just maybe Captain Cub will happen by, and you guys can talk this out?" "OCRAY!" Brian's one word (and Cub's) that we could understand. Well, we wanted to, but we didn't leave him there. So, with the help of his motoring/sailing buddies, we carried him with us. Well not actually carried him, but dragged him through the streets until he finally fell, and there he lay until a local dog couldn't wait to show her love. I never knew you could French kiss a dog!

Well after a little fun entertaining the locals, we head back to the boats. Okay, now "where's the water" when we reach the dinghies? We had dragged the boats so far up the beach, it seems like we are 50 yards away from the nearest water. Yes, we hear some laughing from a few people nearby. Remember this little bit of information when traveling: Never park your boat near a bar that's not on the water!

Finally, about thirty minutes later, we find ourselves in the dinghies and heading back to our sailboats. We look back, and here comes Brian's dog swimming after him. I kid you not! Well, we know that the next morning he will be in a delicate, please-make-no-noise condition. Sorry, pal, not going to happen! No way and not today! So, Steve and I take care of Brian once and for all. We get busy carving out some oranges and other fruits and filling them with anything we can find in our galley. My favorite recipe is flour and maple syrup mixed with a splash of rum and other spices. Armed with our little morning surprise, we load the dingy with our ammunition including some eggs, and motor over to his sailboat. What a pleasant surprise to find him standing in the cockpit and waving as we approach. He doesn't stand a chance when our two armed howitzers unload on him. Another Kodak moment missed! I can't remember if he talked to us that day! But, I kept my job. The dog was not harmed; we made sure she made it back to the island!

Now if you ever get a chance to hang with Brian, this Caribbean dancing, flip-flopping, feather stepping, moonwalking, Mambo King will always keep you laughing! And, if you love to laugh, try listening to one of his jokes for which he never remembers the punch line! But, his attempt is always funnier!

In a few days, we head to Great Guana Cay. To get there requires taking Whale Cay Channel, which means we should head back out to sea around this island to the north. There is absolutely no safe navigation to the south on the bank, especially on a sailboat. And, yep, good old Brian heads that way! Calling and screaming for him not to go there... but Ugh... he goes anyway. The remaining boats just watch in horror, waiting for the bottom to be ripped apart. A few minutes later, Brian calls on the marine radio, "Hey, you guys coming?"

What the heck! Only he could get away with that. We figure he passed through this shallow area at Spring Tide when it reached its maximum height, which occurs only twice each month. The rest of the fleet takes the advice on the chart and heads out the channel. Even the chart was marked in bold letters and highlighted in yellow – "Do Not Attempt Passage." – That means everyone except timely traveler Brian!"

Steve and I go way back. I have known Steve for as long as I can remember, and he remains one of my closest and dearest friends. We have never had a disagreement or argument our entire lives. Not seeing each other for thirty years helped, but I hope that everyone could experience having someone like Steve in her/his life. That person is there for you – always comes running when summoned!

We were both living in Florida during the passing of our mothers, which happened on the same day but different years. I decided that it was a sign from above that Steve and I would die together on the same day: we seldom ride in a car together, and flying together is out of the question.

Our real friendship began back in first grade at a Catholic School, in Meadville, Pennsylvania. You may remember that back in the late 50s and 60s, the school would have someone ring the school bell for the start of the day, lunch, and at other times. Today they call this rather large brass bell an antique. Throughout our Catholic school years, we would have the same teacher that entire school year. The one event that stands out for me was in third grade when I was standing on the school steps screaming. Well, I was saying something when that bell-ringing person stopped mid-bell, and there I was yelling my head off! Now, who was standing right behind me? Yep, my third-grade teacher!

"Come with me, John," she said.

Laughter began probably because everyone knew I would get slapped with that fearful ruler of hers!

"John! I want you to write on the blackboard one hundred times: I will not yell in school."

Back then they had rather large blackboards to write on since they probably didn't have paper and pencils. So, when my teacher left me alone in the room, I quickly used my youthful creative writing skills. I taped, at least, six sticks of chalk to a yardstick and started my task. Boy, this is going well and should finish quickly. I thought! Yes, she was standing right behind me, again!

"John, let me introduce you to my ruler!"

I returned to the Abacos the year after the sailing trip when Cub and I took the DISCOUNT II, a 38' Bayliner Flybridge to the Bahamas. The owner, a well-known car dealer who was often generous with helping others less fortunate (like me); he kept this vessel at our Marina in Sanford. One day, while I was working on his boat, he came up to me and shoved a few thousand dollars into my pocket.

"Hey, look," he said, "have a very good time. Invite some friends and get the boat to Green Turtle Cay in the Abacos, and I'll see you there in about a month."

You see, I maintained and moved his vessel from coast to coast so he could enjoy various areas of Florida. When he shoved the money in my pockets, I wasn't too surprised. Okay, maybe a little!

But, taking the boat to the Abacos was not that simple. To reach the coast from Sanford, you must travel 146 nautical miles north towards Jacksonville before you can enter the Intracoastal Waterway or the inlet to the Atlantic. Cub and I moved the vessel from Sanford up – rather, down (for those who remember that this river flows north) the St. Johns River to Jacksonville. Then we made our way south to Stuart, eventually our Florida departure point. With a morning sunrise and the boat prepared for the crossing, we start out the St. Lucie Inlet.

I notice some rather large rollers coming our way. I go below to tell my girlfriend Lynn to make sure everyone and everything are ready for some rough water ahead.

"Oh, this is calm, Honey!" Lynn replies.

When I point out the forward window to help explain why I am alerting her, she grabs the glass container from the blender and vomits. I didn't see that one coming. You know, we had no frozen drinks made in that blender the entire trip! We are still in calm waters; we haven't even reached the inlet yet! That's the last time she calls me Honey that day!

I first met Lynn while we both worked on a dinner boat back in Sanford. I was this lower middle-class boat captain, while Lynn was working hard and studying mathematical formulations of quantum mechanics. It was love at first sight! I remember walking up to her, shy, scared, and tongue-tied, trying to say something intelligent as if writing a romance novel!

"Lynn, uh I uh was wondering?"

"YES," she replied with the movement of her beautiful blonde hair flowing in the gentle breeze.

"You think later you can explain the De Broglie hypothesis, claiming that all matter, not just light, has a wave-like nature?"

She didn't say a word. She just looked at me with her cold and piercing blue eyes and my confidence was again shattered. The feeling of déjà vu was overwhelming.

To make this long trip seem like the short story that it is— We entered the Bahamas to the north of West End and cruised the shallow waters of the Little Bahama Bank. We made it to Green Turtle Cay by that same evening and once we cleared Customs the next morning, we kicked back and enjoyed the great weather and warm waters of the Abacos. This area in the Bahamas has always been my favorite cruising destination. We ventured east, stopping off at every island.

Several days later, we pull into a marina in Marsh Harbor for fuel and lunch. Their fuel dock is on the T-head, and we have a 20-knot on dock wind! Well, we make it in with no damage to the crew, on-watchers, boats, or my ego. After fueling, I ask if there is somewhere we could dock while we go in town for lunch.

"Sure," says the dock attendant while pointing to the vacant slip.

Now here's where it gets a little tricky. To be able to get off the boat,

I would have to back into the slip instead of pulling in forward, which would be an easier maneuver under these conditions. By backing in, I would have the wind on my beam with a greater chance of damaging the dock, hitting the pilings, gouging the side of the boat, or all the above. So, I pull past the slip and back against the wind to gain a swing momentum before the wind can turn me. The approach technique looked good on paper. I backed in without touching anything to the amazement of several dockhands and fellow boaters.

"We have never seen anyone do what you just did in the wind like that!" said someone.

Well, Mister Big Ego, here, missed the top step of the ladder coming off the flybridge and fell—luckily landing in the dinghy we had stored in the cockpit below.

"Alcohol, that explains how he did it," someone shouted! Shattered for life, again!

If you ever explore the Abacos and if you have read enough of this book to know that I am a trustworthy seaman who could never tell a lie—this is a beautiful area with friendly people. I always loved Green Turtle. I would always stop by there on boat deliveries to fuel and just to say hello to some of the people I have met through the years. Some were from Florida, and I often brought newspapers and magazines for their enjoyment. Years could go by, and I'd arrive, and they always remembered my name. See, being foolish and a good tipper always helps!

CHAPTER 3

Memorable Moments on the Intracoastal Waterway

My cruising friends and I bounced around during the 1980s aboard this 38' Bayliner from Sanford on the St. Johns River to Stuart, then to Tarpon Springs on the West with occasional side trips to the Bahamas. We put many miles on this old girl, but she never let us down. Equipped with a twin Mitsubishi 135hp small diesel, she would finally get up on a plane and run at her top speed of about 16 knots, but only when you exhausted most of the weight from her fuel tanks.

We kept her at a marina in Tarpon Springs for a few months one year. Lynn and I would go over almost every weekend to tinker with the boat. We just enjoyed waking up in the morning and having coffee at the restaurant located right near the docks. While staying aboard the vessel, we would often stop by the famous Sponge Docks for lunch and to visit the many stores along the way. That year our stay in Tarpon Springs went by fast, and it was time for a long trip to bring her back home to Sanford.

We had a crew of about five – no – 4 non-boating friends and myself. A few were very impressed that, while driving, one could watch the little (radar) TV set mounted on the helm. We left the marina about three a.m. Sunday, heading down the Anclote River. I was up on the flybridge to get a better view of the surroundings. As we turned south onto the Intracoastal Waterway, we were suddenly hit with a blinding rainstorm. Not being able to see and the much-needed radar (little TV set on the helm) monitor was at the lower station, I did my best guess estimating to keep her in the channel. Okay, maybe that wasn't my best guess. We found ourselves in ankle deep water once the storm passed, and we had to sit and wait for daylight to assess the damages.

If this would happen today, we could just call a towboat service on our cell phone or VHF marine radio, and they would come to assist. If you are a member, with unlimited towing, there is absolutely no cost to the boater other than the membership fees.

Daylight finally showed up and brought a whole new outlook to my storied career (it might be over). The first thing I said was: "Wow, we're that far out of the channel?" Best guess estimation was maybe 45.72 meters. (You thought I would say 50 yards!) So, then there was Sam, another good friend until after this trip.

I tell Sam: "Take the anchor and go about 20 yards and set it."

"Okay, let me go and get my swimsuit on," he replied.

"Trust me," I assured him, "you probably won't even get your knees wet!"

Sam goes into the water and grabs the steel anchor (with its excellent attached conductor of electricity, the anchor chain) and starts walking.

"Hey," he shouts, "what about the lightning in the area?"

"Sam, the cumulonimbus cloud formation to the west is causing reversing joules disturbance and neutralizing the electrostatic discharge if it strikes the water!" I answered back.

"Oh… Okay," Sam replied.

So, I turned to my uneasy crew and asked: "Do you think he bought that?"

With the anchor set and Sam safely back in the boat, I tried to winch us back to the channel. Now listen, the lightning was way, way off in the distance and Sam was not in harm's way. (Now I wonder if my readers bought that.)

Hey, we're moving! We crawl 19 yards until the winch gives out. With the anchor now safely aboard, I start the engines and dig my way back to the channel in reverse. This vessel's props are somewhat protected because of the bottom design. I can run only about five minutes before the engine will overheat. We would set the stern anchor, and I would go below and clean the sand out of the sea strainers. We do this back-and-forth routine until safely back in the channel.

From there, we head back to the marina to assess any damage to the boat. We take a good look over and find no vibration coming from the props and no overheating from the engines. So, ready to go, we head back out, but by now, at least, eight hours behind schedule.

Headed south along the Intracoastal Waterway, we make it only to Longboat Key, just south of Tampa for the night and to top off her fuel tanks.

We ate well and probably played poker and told jokes before settling in. The next morning, we proceeded south on the Intracoastal Waterway to Ft. Myers where we entered the Okeechobee Waterway and the Caloosahatchee River.

Lake Okeechobee is the largest freshwater lake in the state of Florida and is exceptionally shallow for a lake of its size, with an average depth of only 9 feet. This waterway stretches about 135 nautical miles, and if you enter at Fort Myers, and you make all the right turns, you end up in Stuart. There are three locks west of Lake Okeechobee and two to the east of the lake. I wanted to make the Franklin Lock in Olga and the Ortona lock before nine that night. I don't know the lock schedule now, but back then they closed at 9 p.m., and I wanted to make it to the Moore Haven City docks so we would be ready to enter the third lock at first light and enter Lake Okeechobee.

Now running the waterway at night can be a little scary. I have passed through before, and you hear many strange noises...*unlike* the ones, you hear at the zoo back home. "How about gunshots?" you ask. Yep! A bit worried about the possibility of a stray bullet heading our way, aimed at our bright targeting lights, I was also concerned about swamping small boats or late night fishermen with the wake of our boat. To make up time, I throttled up and had the boat's remote-controlled spotlight aimed at the left river bank, and I asked my brave friend Sam: "Why don't you stand there and shine the handheld spotlight on the right bank?" So, there we are hauling butt through the river, but with me slouching down in my chair just a wee bit.

So, Sam and crew made it safely, without a scratch, to Moore Haven and we secured the vessel to the dock. In such a hurry to get to this point, we had absolutely nothing aboard to eat and nowhere ashore to go. (Ladies, once you let a man drive, that being a car or boat, we don't stop; we just want to get there!) But, my anchor-handling, spotlight-holding comedian buddy found a can of soup. Luckily, for my sake, he found no weapons aboard. He then did his rendition of a commercial where this one can of soup saved the lives of five people on this dark, lonely night. Actually, the soup commercial was funny, and we all laughed ourselves to sleep.

It's morning, and we make our way through the lock at Moore Haven. We're hoping for a calm Lake Okeechobee crossing to the Port Mayaca Lock at the eastern end. With a beautiful calm lake crossing, and no one falling overboard or being thrown overboard, we pass through Port Mayaca, continue to the St. Lucie Lock, and on through the St. Lucie Canal to Stuart.

This is where my crew (now experienced) gets a taste of the St. Lucie Inlet. Remember Lynn and the rollers leaving this inlet from the other chapter? The blender we had to replace? To get where we were going, we had to head out this channel before making our turn to port and hug the shore alongside Hutchinson Island, and all this at night, a rainy night no less. Now we are safely fastened to the marina and the awaiting cars to take us home.

I never knew these guys could run so fast. Who would have thought? Look, there goes Sam with sparks a-flying from the dragging anchor chain still attached to his body! Another friend, Jimmy, rushes away clutching his suitcase with half the clothes hanging out.

"Hey, Jimmy, you dropped your radio!" I yell. There are finger gestures as they entered the cars.

"Hey, guys, wait for me!" I haven't seen these friends ever since! Just kidding!

Okay, none of that last paragraph happened, and some may tell a different story. If you noticed, I didn't mention my other crew that may have been aboard during this trip. But if I had, I would have said something like this person 'probably knows more about the practical aspects of a vessel than I'll ever know.' Also, this person 'would have braved the waters that precipitous morning in Tarpon Springs and left crybaby Sam in the boat!' With that said, I would have had to abandon the part about my 4 non-boating friends concerning the (radar) TV set remark out of the book, which I thought was funny. Did I mention that he also has a brigade of sons, relatives, friends and lawyers that I would have to face if I said anything upsetting about his father or mother in any part of this book? So, Sam, it's all about you!

A few years later I was tied to the same dock at Moore Haven. The results were not the same. The laughter that is! I don't remember the date, but Captain Shawn and I were delivering a wooden vessel from the Crystal River area, via the Okeechobee Waterway and we were at this exact same spot here in Moore Haven. I remember I just finished showering when our ship's master alarm (Shawn Yelling) was activated:

"The boat's on fire!"

"The boat's on fire!"

"The boat's on fire!"

(Our alarm always yelled three times.) Yes, this boat - the one with maybe 200 gallons of gasoline still stored in drums on the top deck. I come flying out of the stateroom and remember it like it was yesterday, except for the date! I was wearing my Lucabaldi designer shirt that said "Paddle Faster: I Hear Banjos!" my light brown Lucabaldi designer boots, cotton-twill baseball cap, and.... OH crap – no pants. "I'll be right back!"

The fire is coming from an electrical panel in the salon, and Shawn is pulling electrical plugs out from the receptacles like grabbing hot marshmallows off their sticks. I pull the engine hatch up, and there she blows! The flames shoot out like an erupting volcano. Once we extinguish the fire, we look at each other, and say, "Screw this!" thinking about walking home. Once we figure out that we are in the middle of nowhere, and hearing a banjo playing nearby, we change our minds!

. Yes, that was another trip we wanted to forget. Once we made it to Stuart, we called the owner and told him where he could find his boat and drove a rental car home.

Even before the fire, we had continuing issues with this vessel. It began to sink offshore as we were heading for Anclote Key, near Tarpon Springs, from our departure port from Crystal River about 55 miles to the north. Yes, the same area where I made my successful and soon-to-be well known (I hope to sell a few books) boat landing. This hasn't been a good spot for me. The boat wasn't handling well, so Shawn went below to check, and he found about three feet of water in the bilge. This boat had about four bilge pumps, but each had about fifty wiring splices using electrical connectors. I'd never seen the likes of this—some, I fear, are not approved for use on a vessel or a car and not on an airplane! So, once repaired the best we could with no tools, we headed to Clearwater for charts. That's right, no tools, no charts, and no engine spare parts.

Soon after our Clearwater departure and just before arriving in Venice, south of Sarasota, we lose the water-cooling pump on one of the engines and must shut it down. I have to maneuver to the dock with the other good engine, which won't remain useful for long after this trip finally ends. So, Shawn fills the water tank while I look for a payphone (a public telephone that is operated by coins or credit card) to make a call to the boat's owner. He tells me that he'll have a new pump for us in Ft. Myers once we arrive there. "Great!" I say, and head back to the boat. The water hose is still in the fill cap, but Shawn is nowhere to be found. I look everywhere and even think he might have fallen overboard and hit his head or something. Boy, do I panic! I run... (Back in those days, I could run. If this would've happened today and I had to go for help, "Sorry, I tried!") I ran back to the marina office for help, only to find him walking back with his head hanging down. He had just received bad news from his family, so everything happening to us on this trip seemed trivial.

A week later (it seemed like a week), we limped into Ft. Myers, and I checked to see if the water pump had arrived. Nothing. So, I called the owner, who decided that we should take the pump off the engine, rent a car and take it to a place in Venice (the place we just came from) to repair the pump. I can't even write what I probably said to him at that moment! I will leave that to the vivid imaginations of my many readers.

Again, we are limping – this time towards Moore Haven – where we decide that once docked, we should barbecue something for dinner, never imagining that we would be the ones almost cooked. The problems continued until we finally made it to Stuart and called it quits.

Do You Remember Scooter from our wonderful pleasure cruise I talked about in Chapter One? What possible reoccurring act of kindness could I bestow upon him and re-experience those few terrible nights in Mexico? It's like when you fall off your bike, and you just can't wait to get back on and try that again. I can do this! Well almost a year later and fresh off our Mexico cruise, I bring you to Saturday, January 20, 1996. (Unlike what I say in Chapter Nine, I do keep a log.)

IT ONLY GETS FUNNIER

What better trip to take Scooter on than crossing the calm waters of Lake Okeechobee as we head towards Moore Haven? Remember, nothing ever happens in Moore Haven. But, the lake was rough that day when I spotted him coming up the ladder to the bridge aboard the 36' Kadey Krogen, one of my favorite boats. This model was the Manatee, and — Are you ready for this? — with only a 280-gallon fuel tank, this vessel has a cruising range of 1,100 nautical miles at 7 knots; drop your speed, and you could stretch that to 1,800 nautical miles. That delivery aboard the slow Manatee from Sanford to Regatta Pointe in Palmetto, Florida, covered 660 miles and took 106 running hours and seven days.

Well, here comes Scooter. Before he enters the bridge, I have my feet propped up on the console, chocolate candy smeared all over my face, and am holding a big bowl of potato chips in my lap.

He walks in, sees chips stuck to my face, and I ask, "What's up, Buddy?"

He looks at me with a sickly frown, turns around, and climbs back down, probably going to the head. Recurring nightmares of Mexico, no doubt. I don't see him the rest of that day.

That evening we anchor east of Fort Myers and settle in for the night. The next morning, we find ourselves in a dense fog having trouble distinguishing all the boats in the area from the navigation markers. As we make our way to the Intracoastal Waterway, about ten boats follow closely behind us since it seems that we have the only radar. It is the first fog bank I ever go through that follows us for almost fifty miles and with windy conditions. About twenty-five miles later we pass under the Boca Grande Causeway. This is where we have our first break. The boats that were following us fly past without even a "Thank you," — our boat just a-rocking from their wakes.

I tell Scooter, "I don't know where they're heading, but the channel doesn't go that way."

Sure enough, the lead boats find themselves grounded. Soon they are back following our slow boat heading north.

In about another twenty miles, we reach Venice, and the fog starts to lift. The parade of boats zooms past again rocking us, but gratefully waving as they go, making our day!

CHAPTER 4

Memorable Moments on the St Johns River

I returned to Stuart after making sure my crew made it safely back to Sanford from Tarpon Springs. I also wanted to ensure that all stories and rumors that were floating about were made up by me! My return was with another crew to help bring the 38 Bayliner the rest of the way back home. I think we had a crew of about five. No, wait – Two: 1 non-boating friend and myself. When we finished, my cruising buddy with me on this trip stopped talking to me. I don't recall ever seeing him again!

We began our trek north after safely passing through the St. Lucie Inlet. After clearing the Port Canaveral area, I asked my friend, Matt, if he wouldn't mind driving for a while? Since this was his first time out on the ocean, I tried to explain what I was doing navigation wise. I tell him, "You have only to stay about two miles off the coast," and showed him how to read the radar and the distance scale and our current compass heading. So, logic would have it that after three minutes of full plotting instructions, we were ready to go: "Just keep a look out for other boats."

Augh...a chance to sleep. But, do you ever get that feeling something isn't right? You know, that feeling when you're trying to sleep in the car, and the person who's driving shouldn't be driving at all? Yes.... That feeling!

A short time later, I flew off the couch when I heard breaking waves, and to my surprise, there was the beach about 200 yards away!

"What The (Insert swear words I may have used. Sorry, keeping true to the story, I must admit I did use bad language here) Are you planning to go for a walk on the beach? Where are you heading?" I yelled.

Matt explained, "Well, I was just following the compass heading you told me to follow."

"Compass heading! What happened to just staying two miles off the coast?"

A short time later, and back on course, we found the fuel dock at a marina just north of St. Augustine. After fueling and a quick dinner, we headed out after dark but stayed on the Intracoastal Waterway. Yes, I let Matt drive from the bridge, but I was safely parked right next to him while trying to get some sleep.

Once again, there was the feeling something wasn't right. It was that same feeling you get when you're on a plane, and you're trying to sleep and then wonder about the pilots. Like if something happens, there's not much you can do about it... Yes... **That** feeling!

We reached a point where the channel goes to the left, and if you continue straight, you will discover that someone strategically placed some rather large boulders on the shoreline. These are the type of rocks that, when you hit them they, never move. I don't know what made me jump up at that moment, but we were just about to test that theory of movement relativity. I grabbed the wheel and pulled hard to port. We cleared just in time, unlike the events in the Titanic movie.

Well, after that turn, I was up and back in command, and Matt went below because he had no problems falling asleep. I made my approach entering the St. Johns River from the ICW. I was sure tired and could use some sleep myself. It was a little cold on the flybridge, so I went below. A short time later, I noticed a mark on the radar screen directly behind us, so I went to the cabin door to check. Nothing! So, I continued. It was pitch black that night. The object kept getting closer and closer, and I continued looking aft but was seeing nothing. Now this possible false echo on the radar is just about to touch us on the screen, so I go to look, and again don't see anything.

I don't remember what made me look up sensing something wasn't right. I could barely see the rather large black-hulled freighter about twenty yards behind us. I must have pulled directly in front of this vessel coming off the ICW onto the river. I was under its radar limits, and they obliviously didn't see my running lights or me. (That's why they're called "running lights": because you're always running away from someone who's bigger than you!) I was fortunate to have an Angel on my shoulder that evening!

Forward through Jacksonville I go, but instead of stopping, I continue. (Ladies, it's a man thing. When you're riding in a car with one of us, you must know we never stop; we just want to get there. I'm the same way when boating.)

It's morning, and I'm up on the bridge, a little hungry and cold and waiting for Matt to come up and relieve me. It's now noon, and I'm still waiting. You can't just put the boat on autopilot and go below because of all the fish traps that litter the channel north of Palatka. It's now late afternoon and no Matt! And believe you me, I can't tell you how often I was jumping up and down on the deck to try to wake him. By the time I got home (probably late evening), I had to go inside his cabin to wake him.

When you run the river, with the many Slow Speed areas and Manatee Protection Zones, you can't be in a hurry. But back during the time of this voyage, there were no such restrictions. Me that day? Pushing the limits of the boat, I wasn't slowing down for no one. So, let's see, how many hours was I on this wheel without sleeping? 32-hours!

I made up for that slow time a few years later when I was to deliver a 39' Sea Ray coming from the Bahamas to Lighthouse Point near Pompano Beach. Another friend ... and I don't quite remember who went with me that trip; it could've been Shaun, but not Capt. Shawn; or maybe it was Sam? I'll just call him Jimmy. Nope, it had to be Shaun. Anyway, if it was Shaun, we were still friends and began our move north to Sanford. I had been told all was well with the vessel. The boat looked good; all systems were in working and in serviceable condition.

If you ever go looking to buy a boat, remember the term "serviceable." This means if an engine, part or accessory, can be serviced or repaired, it's serviceable. If the survey says "Not in working or serviceable condition," that means you now have only another working anchor.

So, now we're ready to get this Sea Ray to Sanford. We have two choices and two choices only: run at idle speed or full throttle, but nothing between. The propellers were so bent up, this vessel performed at those two speeds; anything else and the vibration would remove any fillings you had in your mouth.

At throttle UP, we motor out the Hillsboro Inlet at about 7 a.m. and make a left turn, pointy end heading in a northerly direction. We reach a marina in Saint Augustine for fuel, dinner, and an evening layover. The next morning, all speed records are about to be broken: Departing at 6 a.m. and sitting at the railroad bridge at Lake Monroe in Sanford by 5 p.m. that same day, we would've been there sooner if not for a few wrong turns on the river! Fishermen just love us! The boat's huge wake launches fish airborne and drop them right into their boats. I see a guy sitting out on his porch as I propel a good one and knock him right out of his chair. The fishermen have our backs today if the law enforcement boats are out! CB-like chatter on the marine radio is everywhere:

"Break 1-9 for that southbound boat-eating-cheesecake (that was us); how's it lookin' on your donkey?"

"10-4," I reply. "There was a plain brown wrapper at the 82 stick, a bear in the air working the Lilly Pads!"

"Boat-eating-cheesecake, you're clear to the 101 stick. I'm waiting for my real catch."

I just love it when I make this stuff up! Okay, I never knocked anyone off his chair or swamped any boats, and did make it safe to Sanford. I didn't have a CB radio aboard or harm any fish! But, boy, was that fast!

If you ever get to visit the St. Johns River, you're in for a pleasurable journey. Remember, you can't be in a hurry either. The St. Johns River is one of the safest and easiest gateways from the Atlantic Ocean. Between Mayport and Sanford, the river is an enjoyable cruise.

To Sanford, overhead clearance is set at 45 feet by three fixed bridges. Snags are seldom a problem in the main channel, but side streams and sloughs should be approached carefully. Be observant from November through March, when manatees are in residence. The current south of Palatka can be influenced by the water level in the upper (southern) part of the river, as is flows south to north.

The St. Johns is the longest river in Florida - 310 miles long. It is one of the few rivers in the United States that flows north. The source of the river, or headwaters, is a large marshy area in Indian River County that flows north and turns eastward at Jacksonville to its mouth in the Atlantic Ocean. The total drop of the river, from its source in swamps south of Melbourne to its mouth in the Atlantic near Jacksonville, is less than 30 feet, or about one inch per mile, making it one of the "laziest" rivers in the world. Major tributaries or smaller streams and rivers that flow into the St. Johns River includes the Wekiva River, Econlockhatchee River, and the Ocklawaha River. Florida waters are often a natural brown tea color caused by tannins from decaying native vegetation. Since light is attenuated by both color and turbidity, Secchi depth in many Florida lakes is often very shallow compared to water bodies in other parts of the world.

So if you ever get the chance to visit this amazing river and make it to Sanford, you'll be surprised at the three area marinas and what each offers the visiting boater. Or, just stay for a while. You'll have a choice of the Boat Tree Marina at the Port of Sanford just before entering Lake Monroe, or Monroe Harbour Marina at the City's downtown riverfront, or Sanford Boat Works just east of Lake Monroe.

Not everything memorable has happened to me at sea. Remember, I work at a marina where the term "Not in serviceable condition" probably got its name. Which brings me to our old Travelift and the fall day in 1971 when I got my first look at this twenty-ton beauty. What a gem! This one wasn't like the newer self-propelled lifts you see today, but one pulled by a 1920s truck, which for the first few years I was working there never ever had water or engine oil. Never! It only moved back and forth some 50 yards and the engine would run for only about ten minutes. But, come on now – no oil or water? Which brings me to one more focus topic – our Marina Maintenance Program!

One day, we looked at it - our yellow crappy-looking travel lift. How's about we clean it up with a nice wash down. We added water, a new oil filter, and some fresh oil. Boy, did we feel good about this! We even touched up the body with a new coat of yellow, and when finished, we stepped back and marveled at our now newer-looking and well-maintained travel lift. The next day the engine blew up! I think we canceled the Marina Maintenance Program immediately after that.

CHAPTER 5
My First Distress Call

Out and about working around the marina since 1971, I sure have stockpiled many stories to tell, for a later day or another book. Yes, why not embarrass some more of my friends. But, before I get to all those memorable events with pictures, we still must deliver a new dinner boat to Florida back in 1983.

Chesapeake Shipbuilding of Salisbury, Md., was awarded the contract with Star Line Corporation of Williamston, Michigan, to design and build a full-service restaurant vessel. Construction brought forth the 122-foot STAR OF SANFORD to be placed into service at the downtown riverfront on the Lake Monroe part of the St Johns River. With a seating capacity of 400 and a full galley capable of preparing all meals onboard, the STAR OF SANFORD was to replace the first dinner boat in Sanford: the BAY QUEEN.

We now had to get a crew and go to Maryland and bring the STAR OF SANFORD to Florida. If I remember, we had a team of about six and my trusted Cubby just shy of receiving his license. After checking out the boat on our arrival at the shipyard, we left Maryland and ventured down the river to the Chesapeake. Our first run was down the winding Wicomico River some 24 nautical miles to the Chesapeake Bay, then pass quietly through the Norfolk Naval Base under watchful eyes before deciding to use the Dismal Swamp Canal. From there we passed through Albemarle Sound and into Pamlico Sound before exiting the Intracoastal Waterway at Wilmington, North Carolina, and on to Jacksonville to enter the St Johns River.

We were about 20 miles off the coast, and I just came to the bridge to relieve the on-watch captain sometime late evening. The bridge was about 10' wide or more, and I was positioned on the port side at the chart table checking our position when a storm hit and a rogue wave picked the boat up and tossed us like a toy dinghy. I flew across the bridge without touching the floor and landed on the starboard side entrance door. I was so fortunate that that door was closed, or out I would've gone without saying goodbye. The other captain altered course to take the waves off the port quarter, but that meant heading away from Jacksonville and going farther out to sea. When another crashing wave hit us, we found the second deck windows almost wave height, and it was at that moment I made my first distress call.

The Coast Guard responds and I give our current position, heading, and speed and request that they are on alert of our situation if assistance is needed. By now all crew is on the bridge waiting for me to plot a course so we can turn the vessel to take the waves off the starboard bow and head for the protection of Jacksonville. Looking down the row of men worried and concerned as I am, I give the order,

"180 degrees to port," and turn her into the wind—thankful I had paid attention to plotting in school. I notify the Coast Guard when we reach the safety of the St Johns River – to the delight of all aboard. Below, all the refrigeration equipment we had secured is stretched to almost the breaking point as ready to be launched through the windows.

While the STAR operated lunch, dinner, and charters out of Sanford for a few years, this vessel offered daily entertainment, and had a galley crew of about 8, with bartenders, and dining staff with a complement of two officers and four deckhands. The STAR was always alive with entertainment to the delight of the many passengers, but one cruise stands out in memory: I wanted to play a prank on our loveable chef. Another staff captain was aboard at the time, and I have him take the helm while all six of us go down to the first deck for dinner. All the passengers are up on the second deck watching the show or dancing, so we are there all by ourselves. He comes out of the galley and looks at all of us while mentally counting the crew and, in a panic, he asks, "AH, who's driving the boat?"

Well, we look at each other with terror-filled faces and run up the stairs leaving him just standing there in shock. I don't remember if he ever talked to me after that?

Another prominent memory (but not one of my finest moments) – we were just coming in off the lake in the afternoon. To offset the high winds, I was coming into the marina faster than my usual slow-as-you-go approach. The area just outside the marina has a depth of about 18 feet, the highest in Lake Monroe, and at the entrance channel, it suddenly shallows to about 7 feet. Well, with the increased speed and upon reaching the shallower water, I felt the boat lift. The rapid rising of the vessel altered my course to starboard. I was heading right to the shore with no response from steerage. The only thing I could do to avoid an unscheduled beach landing was put the engines in reverse.

Well, the boat stopped for sure, but I had no control of the port engine. At least, we were drifting away from the beach. I had one of the deck hands go below to check the engine room. The crew member comes up in a panic and tells me there's no port shaft. I can't even remember my reaction or what I said. I knew once we docked the boat was going back out on a charter in a few hours. I limped in on one engine and saw the facial expression from one of the managers as I came below to check the damages.

The good news if any was that I damaged the rubber disc vibration damper between the prop shaft and transmission. The shaft coupler just dropped about three feet and bottomed out at the thru-hull connection. This device is designed to shear away if striking a submerged object to protect the transmission from damage. So, we winched the shaft up and bolted the flange to the transmission so we could, at least, use the engine to maneuver inside the marina. Everything ended up well until I found out how much that little part costs – with constant reminders from the owners.

A few years later Star Line would leave the St Johns River. So, with the company a fond memory, the original operators of the BAY QUEEN leased a vessel called RIVERSHIP ROMANCE a wide-bodied catamaran type vessel just shy of 110 feet.

The family operated this boat for a few years until another *lady* that would become the undisputable queen of the river with the GRAND ROMANCE a 136-foot, triple-decked excursion vessel brought into service in 1989. Designed by John Brever, an associate of Florida Naval Architects, Inc. of East Palatka, the 600-passenger vessel was constructed by Freeport Shipbuilding & Marine Repair and had an amazing 46-foot beam to help add to here massive presence despite only having a shallow 4' 6" draft.

I always enjoyed my time aboard this grand *lady*. It was returning to the dock with a strong wind coming from the east or west that had you worried! I can't forget about a south wind too, but a north wind was good! These directional barriers often brought the elements of fear and excitement for the captain and crew, all within 30 seconds! The docking maneuver that offers a small margin of error and an excellent chance of embarrassment, for me, was like being in the Twilight Zone. The crew had a better name for it and dedicated "Blunder Basin" in my honor. If I had a rough docking that night, I could get back at the crew with my weekly radio talk show – *Doctor Driver* if they made any distressing comments! No one was safe during this tell-all talk show! I made up stories about everyone! So, instead of laughter, I would hear,

"great docking – the wind sure shook the entire boat – must have been a 20 knot Nor'easter!"

On one occasion (Annette, you will love this one), one of the nice features aboard this vessel is the ability to maneuver at different locations. You have the option to walk out onto the bridge wing, about 18' from the pilothouse and control the boat from there with a complete view of the side. This makes it easier to dock if you aren't scared of heights. It also gives you the opportunity of not having to rely on your judgment for distance or someone telling you're ten feet from the dock pilings when you're only two feet right before you smack right into them! Throughout my career, I hit the pilings only fifty-two times: all my contacts with pilings have been nothing more than gentle bumps with an occasional minor bruise to my ego! I still hold the marina record for the biggest ego! This boat is equipped with an electric Micro Commander Control System and, to take control of the engines, you must push a button at any of the three stations.

Well, Annette was aboard one-night visiting and showing off her new glamor shot pictures, and if I remember right, it was cold and raining. Annette was wearing my yellow hooded raincoat since I didn't much care to mess up my always trimmed and flowing dark hair. I was making my usual slow approach from the pilothouse when about 100 yards from the dock I walked out on the wing with a slight right rudder on. When I pushed the button to take control, Nothing! No power or control of the engines. So, I moseyed (ran) back inside and when I pushed the button inside the pilothouse I could gain control of only the starboard engine. The port engine would've been nice to have in this situation, not the starboard, as my momentum was sliding me closer to port and a parallel dock loaded with boats.

So, I had Annette stand out on the wing to give me distances while everyone below thinking that was me, but a much taller me, standing up there, just yelling away as I just missed damaging all the boats with my sliding big butt stern by just a foot. (I think I started drinking after that trip!) Also at the marina on that cold and windy night were Shawn and Scooter standing on the dock to catch our heaving line. The toss fell short, and when Shawn reached down to grab it, the floating dock moved; he lost his footing and into the water he went. His Flying Squirrel dive met with a wet smack down! When watching, it seemed evident that a forward 3-1/2 in the tuck is harder than a Squirrel dive, so he never received an honorable mention on my *Doctor Driver* show; I was waiting for the book release!

The times and dinner boats have changed throughout the years, and the founding family eventually sold the business to another local family operator. A second vessel also named RIVERSHIP ROMANCE, operated on the St Johns River for many years but stopped cruising a few years back.

Today when you visit this beautiful riverfront community of Sanford you'll still find me standing about or power napping in my office. But, ashore away from my loud snoring sounds you can visit a vibrant historic downtown district with its many shops, restaurants and beautiful architecture that comes alive at night with many monthly activities including their well know "Alive after Five" held on the second Thursday of every month. Also, a must see on the beautiful Riverwalk is the BARBARA-LEE, an authentic sternwheel paddleboat docked at the marina and operated by the original family members who started it all and captained by Shawn.

Photograph by: Robin McClain
Captain "Shawn"

The family includes Bill, Debbie, and Captain John – who grew up on the dinner boats – are giving it a go, under the name the St. Johns Rivership Co. and are doing well these last few years. Captain John usually cruise directs, and I promise you this – he's one humorous and entertaining director, just like his father on the Grand and RIVERSHIP ROMANCE.

The 350-person boat, with its big windows overlooking the paddle, is a view back in time and adjusts well with the history of the St. Johns River. The steel hull is propelled by two paddle wheels at the rear of the vessel. The wheels can turn forward or backward independently of each other, allowing the ship to maneuver easily in tight quarters. The 105-foot ship, built in 1986 was extensively refurbished before entering service in Sanford. The ornate wrought iron railings and wooden wheels recall the elegance of the steamers that once plied the St. Johns River between Jacksonville and Sanford.

The BARBARA-LEE is well set-up. You can charter part or all of the ship for weddings, birthdays, anniversaries, family reunions, business meetings, and other special events. The ship features an open-air top deck, a covered "paddlewheel deck" overlooking the wheels, an enclosed upper deck that seats 60 diners with its own dance floor. Also, a mezzanine deck that seats 40 and the large main salon deck that seats 84 and has a bar, stage, and dance floor. The enclosed dining areas are climate controlled with air conditioning and heating.

Photograph by: John Sternberg
http://www.stjohnsrivershipco.com

CHAPTER 6
Charter Fishing Trip

There's nothing like the open sea, blue skies, and saltwater fishing. Okay, let's talk about this for a moment. You remember my friend Steve, yep, the let's-lock-up-the-Spanish-teacher, my Bahamas sailing buddy friend? So, we're fishing on one of the marina docks in Sanford when we catch a Speckled Perch. Now the fish is flopping around all over the dock, and we're arguing who's going to take it off the hook because he knew I couldn't! Well, this little girl standing nearby walks over and removes the hook from the fish. I can't remember when Steve ever stopped laughing! That's how much I like to fish. The fear is called Ichthyophobia, so I always bring my welding gloves just in case that girl isn't around!

One day I get this call from another friend of mine, Jim, who's on the marina's softball team.

"Hey, Luke, we chartered a fishing boat over at Ponce Inlet, and one of the guys can't make it. So, are you in?"

The macho king fisherman, deep sea, rough water guy and later a fighting ninja warrior just comes out of me, and I say,

"YES." Flashback to that Speckled Perch I landed with Steve a few years before. What the hell am I thinking!?

I don my brand new $30 white Reebok sneakers and drive to Ponce Inlet on the east coast. We load up the chartered (only six-passenger) boat and head out to sea to catch that big game fish. When you charter a boat, you don't do much but stand around, catch sun and drink. I just call it like it is – The Immaculate Consumption! The boat's mate does all the rigging, and you sit comfortably in the fighting chair. Then, it's finally my turn, and I hook a sailfish! The excitement is so loud I can't hear what the mate's saying. But I think it goes like this:

"Dude, I haven't seen a sailfish that big in years! Make a decision—catch or release?"

"What?" I ask.

"Do you want to keep the fish and mount it or release it?" The sales job is now embedded in my shattered mind, and I don't want to keep it.

"Well, hell.... release it...." And then the Jimmy influence kicks into high gear!

"Oh, man, you got to mount this sailfish! Just look how big it is!"

I reply, "Well, Jim, you sit here, and you bring it in..."

"Oh no, buddy, it's all yours. You hooked it!" ... as he spills beer all over me!

Now the mate is telling me the procedures and costs if I keep it, and my brain is working overtime to figure out how much per inch, how much deposit for the taxidermist, etc. I'm just hoping this soon-to-be-expensive fish I'm about to catch would just fall off the hook. After hours of heart pounding labor, it is finally mine. Okay, maybe twenty minutes of heart pounding work just in case one of the other guys on the boat reads this!

Well, into the boat goes my fish and it's jumping all over the place. The decision is made – *mount* it! So, the day reaches mid-afternoon. The captain alters course, and we head back to shore. I watch as the first mate raises the sailfish flag indicating our catch. (Correction: My expensive prize-catch!) Let me see, my new Reebok sneakers cost me $40; my part of the charter about $200, and the fish deposit to mount about another $200. (Oh boy, I wasn't counting on this at all.)

I now see Jim talking to the captain with that shit-eating grin of his. 'Well, I'm a captain of a sort,' I say to myself. 'So, what is he up to? Oh, I know, they probably throw me into the water once we dock or create some other embarrassing event. Oh, that's what You think, pal...' The marina where this vessel is docked has one of the most popular restaurants on site, and when we arrive, the docks are packed with curious onlookers. So, what do I do to protect myself from their little surprise attack? I Grab their wallets, cameras, and whatever else I can find and stuff them into my pants and shirt. Now, these guys are over six feet tall, and we all play on the same softball team. They easily just pick me up, strip me down, and throw me—and my new $50 Reebok sneakers—overboard in front of everyone! Everyone! I can't get my ego out of the water fast enough! Just shake it off and laugh with the rest. I enjoy being in the water if someone else jumps in first. That's my Early Warning Testing for Sharks-in-the-water protocol.

Now dried and clothed again, I'm told to help hold the fish I caught so they can take pictures.

"You're asking me to touch this fish?" and here I am without my welding gloves!

"Well, you caught it!" they reply.

Immediate fear takes me back again to that small speckled perch we caught on the docks in Sanford. Okay....so here I am...the big game fisherman, cautiously holding up the tail fin and hoping it doesn't move, because if it wiggles I'm done for and I can never show my face around here again!

Okay, I survived. I was a little bummed afterward because the boat crew didn't use the fish I caught to be mounted. I should've just released it because you have only to tell the taxidermist you want a rather large sailfish mounted and facing left. Yes, you can say: "I caught that!"

CHAPTER 7

My Three Captains!

There's nothing like the open sea, blue skies, and saltwater fishing. You know, I think I said that before. With the smell of fish and my joy of the fishery still fresh in my mind, Cub, Shawn and I decide to go fishing off Canaveral on the east coast of Central Florida. On this memorable day, we take the marina's 21' center console fishing boat. Cub picks us up with his jeep to tow the boat to the east coast. We stop at one of the tollbooths as we near Canaveral. None of us have any change with us, so Cub flies right thru without paying. "You know, Cub, this might come back and haunt us one day for not paying," I say, not thinking that would be today!

Arriving at the Cape, we buy some bait and head for the public launching ramp. With the gear loaded, we back down the steep ramp... a little too fast: we almost sink the boat! Water is flowing over the transom and into the cockpit, giving this boat its first taste of saltwater. So back out of the water she goes to drain some of the water before slowly launching her again. Slowly we go! We are now safely floating and with the jeep parked, off we go! Hey, we're moving; how safe can this be? We're all excellent captains, except if we have to back a boat down a ramp!

So now we're out about three miles offshore, soaring up and down against the waves just like in *Miami Vice* back in the day but with a smaller, cheaper, crappier-looking center-console boat.

Cub asks, "Hey, where's the cooler?"

"What cooler?"

"The one with the snacks, drinks, my wallet and the car keys!"

"Oh boy, that cooler!"

We think, at first, it might have fallen out of the boat from one of the waves I hit, so we motor slowly back to see if it was floating but find nothing. Well maybe we left it back at the dock, so back we go. Nothing again, nowhere. We ask a few fishermen at the launching ramp if they have seen a white cooler.

"No," they reply. (I'm sure there are a few honest fishermen!)

"Well," Cub offers, "we came all this way; let's go back out, get some fishing in, and we'll call someone when we get back and have them bring out the spare car keys." On our way out again, at about that dreadful three-mile-offshore mark, I'm performing more of my airborne acts of terror when Cub falls back and knocks the VHF marine radio off his belt clip, and into the water, it goes.

Back in those days, nothing ever seemed to float—except for the cooler Cub brought labeled on the side "It even floats!" So, there's the possibility there wasn't an honest fisherman back at the ramp that day!

Be not discouraged, fish, we're still coming for you. We continue until another wave hits and launches us airborne. There goes the Loran, the instrument that tells us why we're not lost! Still not discouraged, we venture out into deeper waters and fish. Have I mentioned that all of us suck at fishing, except Cub and Shawn?

"Fish On..." we all yell and what a struggle! We fight that fish for hours (12 minutes), each of us taking a turn reeling it closer to the boat. In she comes with typical bouncing about, teeth a-grinning and blood flying everywhere. What do they do with this mean looking Kingfish? They chase me around the boat with it for hours (2 minutes), and I'm screaming my head off.

So, with my sore throat from telling too many jokes, we decide it's time to head back. It's been a fun day with some good friends and another fish tale to tell my grandkids when they're born twenty-something years from now. Well, we're at the boat ramp. I stay with the boat while Cub and Shawn make for a phone booth (Do you remember those?) to make a call for extra keys. "What's that?" you ask when they return. "The phone booth service was not working," so they had to walk a few miles to town to make the call.

So, yes, they left me behind to watch the boat and the gear, what few items were left. Well, later, maybe around midnight, the spare keys show up. We head for Sanford. Do you remember the tollbooth I mentioned earlier in the day? Well, we're right back at another one, and without batting an eye, Cub pulls over, gets out of the Jeep, removes everything from his pockets, and throws it all into the toll collection slot.

"Hey, Cub, you didn't throw the car keys in by chance?"

You know, we almost got away with it. If only that state trooper didn't show up! Okay, he didn't throw the keys in the collection slot, but when the officer pulled up, we just told him that's how we found the damaged tollbooth!

Ah Yes, the Loran Navigation System we had aboard before losing it—that's how far back this voyage dates us. Navigational time periods go something like this: Lucky-Guess-Navigating-Dead-Reckoning period (2750 BC-1940), the Loran-Period around 1974 (1940-1995), and the GPS-Navigating-Systems era (1995-).

I remember my trip to the Bahamas as a rookie. During the (extended-for-those-lacking- money) Lucky-Guess-Navigating-Dead-Reckoning-Period I found myself aboard a vessel owned by a congressman. We were joined by a 49' Alaskan trawler, owned and operated by Ray Kauffman. Ray, who kept his boat in Sanford during the winter, wrote *Hurricane's Wake, Around the World in a Ketch*, back in 1940. One winter Ray was heading back to the Bahamas and wanted to know if I would like to help a couple who also kept their boat in Sanford. "Absolutely," I said and off we went. Now, Ray (in the early 70s) with no navigational equipment aboard other than a radio directional finder, could hit his waypoints dead-on, anytime and anywhere. Yes, I was that impressed with his knowledge of the sea: just sitting down to dinner and listening to his stories kept me in awe!

This was the first time I entered Miss Emily's Blue Bee Bar in New Plymouth on Green Turtle, and I placed my business card on the left wall when you entered her place. This was also the first time I ever left the USA.

After about a week, I parted ways as the two vessels continued their trip through the Bahamas. I took a water taxi from Green Turtle to Treasure Key and my awaiting prop plane sitting on the tarmac. Ray reminded me, whatever I do, get on that plane because they shut down the airport once the plane leaves and he would have already left the area. So, there I sat looking forward to my first airplane ride. When it was time to board, we had to walk out to the plane, maybe 100 yards away from this small terminal. As I approached, I noticed oil dripping from one of the engines. I thought maybe this was why they didn't pull up to the terminal so no one could see and try to get their money back. Even though I was concerned, I boarded because I was told this airline has never had an accident in the three weeks they had been flying. From Treasure Key, we had to fly to Marsh Harbour, just a few miles away, to pick up more passengers and probably an extra quart of oil. The next thing I knew; the plane was flying through a brush fire from the ground! So, let's recap - first plane ride, do not like heights of any kind, don't smoke, and my desire to become a pilot—or to ever fly again—comes to an end!

CHAPTER 8
Sailing—What Was I Thinking?

I have had the pleasure of many boating adventures, but they were all on someone else's boat. Since I couldn't afford a nice trawler, I set my sights on a sailboat. Yes, a sailboat. It was in the winter of 1999. I found a bank that just listed a repossessed 1989 30' Hunter in Jacksonville. So, off I went to check her out. It was docked at a marina on the Ortega River. An employee was taking me to the docks, and we walked past many boats. I was saying to myself; "Wow... I hope it's that one... No, this one, or maybe that one..." until we finally stopped. Here she is, and my new love was bowed in; she looked like a little battleship but without the rigging. I just loved the look and the hull design, and with an 11-foot beam, she had a spacious interior.

I couldn't wait to get back to call and make an offer before someone else did. The next day I called the bank to ask how much they would take. I told them the boat looked like it needed a ton of work to put her back in shape! OK, I lied about the repairs, but the negotiations were on and back and forth we went until we settled on a price.

Now, back to Jacksonville for a haul-out and survey. I was on the boat when someone from the boat next to me popped his head up from inside his cabin.

"Hey!" I said to another boat person.

"Hello," he replied.

"Can I ask you something?"

"Sure," he said.

"I'm buying this boat and want to know if the mast is supposed to be bent like this?" I remember his response!

"Well, you're buying this boat, and you have no (insert swear word here) idea what you're looking at?"

"Ah, kind of.... Sorry I asked!"

The next thing was to start the engine and head over to the slip to have her hauled and inspected. Other than the barnacles on the bottom and a little cleaning inside and out, the engine and boat looked brand new. The Yanmar 16hp diesel was all I needed to use this boat as my economy trawler, but with the mast up (that I found out later was a racing design), she was 50-foot-tall off the water and raked aft for speed.

Well, since the bridges on the St. Johns River had a clearance of only 45 feet, I had the mast lowered and hauled back by truck to Sanford where I put her in shape. I named her APPARENT WIND. She was wing keeled and drew only a little over 4 feet. I threw everything that I could afford on her, including radar, autopilot, GPS, new radios, bilge pumps, the works! I even bought the book, *Sailing for Dummies*. The pictures were most helpful!

I was sailing her in Lake Monroe, but now it was time to get her feet wet in saltwater, so I arrange to have her hauled to a marina over near the coast one summer. I arrived on a Friday and walked up to the marina's office counter. The dockmaster at the time was standing there. "Hello," I began, "I just wanted to let you know that my boat is outside to be unloaded." I placed my business card on the counter and slid it to him. He picked it up and slung it back. I looked around to make sure I wasn't, by chance, on *Candid Camera*.

"Sorry," I tried again. "I just wanted to let you know I was here."

"Well, you'll just have to wait!" He said in his raised voice.

So, I wait and wait and apologize to my friend for the delay because if his truck is not moving, he's not making any money. Finally, we head to the Travelift area to offload, and they gently place her in the water. They have the crew from the marina yard down on the boat with me to raise and rig the mast, and the crane operator is yelling his head off to his helper.

"Son," I say, "don't listen to him; you listen to me. This is my boat, and you must attach the forward stay first, or whatever a real sailor calls that part of the rigging, or you can't rig this mast. Trust me." The crane guy finally leaves us alone and up the mast goes as planned.

So, now I'm sitting at the fuel dock waiting for a slip assignment just as the dockmaster shows up.

"Now listen, you. I can put you in that slip over there, but I want you out of here by Friday."

"Just wait a minute, please!" I reply. "I made all these arrangements in advance and even told you that I will be leaving Tuesday, so what seems to be your problem?"

(I'm just saying....)

So, I give him a brand new $50 bill for a tip. What the hell was I thinking? Later that day, he's a little richer and bit friendlier, so I talk about coming back here after my trip, in about two weeks. I'll need a slip for a few days until I can arrange to get the boat back to Sanford? "Absolutely," he says in a calm, polite voice.

Well, Tuesday is here, and another friend is aboard for the trip. With boat loaded and fueled we start out the inlet. Wouldn't you know—at that very moment—my depth sounder stops working! I'm not too concerned since I've been to all the places we're heading; I'm more concerned with the GPS navigator since it was just installed and I haven't had time to test the accuracy of the unit.

Naturally, a rough weather day and night set in, and we finally limp into Ft. Pearce. In need of rest and repairs at the city marina, we stay a few nights. The departure morning comes, and since the weather is still too bad offshore, we motor down and stay the night at a marina in North Palm Beach before making the crossing to the Bahamas. You know how you get when you're tired? How you just don't have the strength? And you just want to go to bed? Well, at the fuel dock, I'm on the boat's swim platform, and I grab the wrong handrail. I grab the stern ladder. Into the water, I go—clothes and all.

"Sir, are you okay?" asks the attendant.

"Look, it's hot as hell out, and the dip felt good. I just want to go to my slip, plug in the shorepower, and turn on the air conditioning." The dock is large enough, but I can't reach the electrical outlet, so here we sit, dripping with sweat all night.

The next morning, we leave Palm Beach Inlet, sails up and heading south. I want to get past Miami before turning towards the Bahamas to help offset the north flowing Gulf Stream. It's early afternoon, and we haven't even made it to Miami. I tell Michael, this is crazy! We should head to the Bahamas now." We do, and it gets so rough out in the stream this brave captain started to worry. This is the first time I actually used "brave" in this entire book.

With the sails lowered and the GPS indicating we were 35 nautical miles north of West End on Grand Bahama Island, we entered the Little Bahama Bank at night, where the water is 20 or so feet deep. I shined the spotlight, and sure enough, shallower water. Who needs a depth sounder, and the GPS seems accurate?

Let's see, we've been at the helm for about 24 hours, and as daylight comes, we raise the sails and shut down my tiny little motor so it can get some rest. Mike is now keeping a watch while I try to sleep. It's still windy (about 15-20 knots) and out of the east. With this autopilot, you have only to push a button, and it will take you from a starboard tack to a port tack without touching the helm.

Later that day, Mike is down checking out the chart. I enjoy showing him how to read and plot during our voyage.

He comes up and says, "You should come down and look where we are."

I kid you not! In the last four hours, we have made no headway. We're probably further back than where we started sailing.

Yep! Sails came down, and the engine starts. We motor and arrive at Great Sale Cay around 7 that evening. Great Sale Cay is an excellent protective area to stay. It takes only 12 hours to go 50 nautical miles once on the Little Bahama Bank. I drop the anchor and don't even remember if I made it back to the cabin after 35 hours of non-stop pleasure boating. Blazing Speed! You should go out and buy a sailboat for yourself! Okay, just wait a minute! If I had bothered to learn how to sail, I'd quit blaming the boat for my lack of sailing skills. Telling it as it was, I was a power boater using as a trawler a sailboat that has only a 16hp motor!

The next morning, we round Great Sale and head east towards Green Turtle Cay. An enjoyable and long ride, we make there at sunset. The anchorage off Green Turtle is crowded with sailboats due to a regatta going on. So, we head to my friend's marina and pull into a slip at the end of the dock. Someone from a nearby boat walks over and says, "Hello!"

I replied: "Is William around?"

"Well," he answers, "he's retired, and his son is running the marina, but I think he's up at the house."

"Is there a place I can tie my boat up for the evening?"

He replies, "Just stay here for the night."

So, with APPARENT WIND fastened to the dock, I head up, and sure enough, there's Bill; we sit and chat for hours (15 minutes) talking about old times back in the States.

"Hey, Bill," I say, "I have to clear Customs in the morning. What time does their office open?"

"If he didn't stay on the mainland last night, probably around nine," was the answer.

I head back to the boat for some good old American made Air Conditioning shipped from China and some much-needed rest. The morning comes, and I have the great pleasure of meeting Bill's Bahamian dockmaster, Albert. No hello, just...

"WT (he did use a swear word here) are you doing here? And why are you still flying that quarantine flag at my marina?"

"Well, I haven't cleared Customs yet and...." In his raised and terrifying voice, he yells:

"You haven't cleared Customs yet?"

Then in a just-shy-of-screaming voice, he continues:

"Now get over to the Customs Office and haul that yellow flag down now! And, besides, I have someone going in your slip where you're at now, and it's the only space I have."

"Well, do you want me to move?"

"No," he answers. "Just stay there for now and get to town and clear Customs."

So, off I go down the path of pure happiness, and I find myself in the Customs Office without my glasses. Sure enough, I feel back-to-back screaming heading my way. This is where creative thinking pays off.

I don't want to have to walk back to the boat, so I say: "Sir, I had a bad night getting here, even lost my glasses, and I can't see a thing on your forms."

"Well, Captain, let me see if I can't fill this out for you and get you on your way so you can enjoy your stay in my beautiful country.

I will give you a piece of advice: when you finally make it to Panama in fifteen years, this won't always be the case and Customs may not be as friendly as I am."

"Ah, thank you," I react with a puzzled look!

(As you continue reading, you'll sense the author has some serious issues to address and should try to keep true to the story.)

"I see from your diploma that you have a degree in Parapsychology?" I ask.

"Yes, he answers, and I just finished writing my book, *Clairvoyance, The Ease of Planning Ahead*.' You see, I have already read the book you're going to write when you get back from Panama!" Still mystified, I shake his hand with a brand new $50-dollar bill that he knew he was getting. I would've given him $100 if I didn't need the extra cash when I reach Panama like he said!

I rush back to see Albert, who waits patiently for his brand new 50-dollar bill. A short time later—we are now best of friends: "Hey, Albert, I'm going to head to Marsh Harbour; then work our way back here in a few days. Any chance for a slip for a night on my return?"

"Absolutely, my wealthy American friend!"

We hang out for the day and spend another night, and by now I'm a regular at Miss Emily Blue Bee Bar. Also, I count, at least, two hardware stores and an ice crème parlor. Life is looking good all over again.

CHAPTER 9

I'm Still Sailing – Days Later

The next morning, we depart for Marsh Harbour. And, believe you me, if we were heading anywhere the next day, that's precisely the direction from which our daily 25-knot winds would blow. Yes, blowing at us every single day. So, we head out Whale Cay Channel to the north and now have the protection of the island.

"Hey," Mike says, "look how nice it is, and the winds have finally died down!"

"Just wait till we get past this island, then see if you want to repeat what you just said," I reply.

Once making Whale Cay, we can barely make headway in the channel. I tell Mike, "Look, I'm not going to take another day to reach Marsh Harbour twelve miles away, so let's go to another place I know and get out of this weather."

So, I call the marina on the VHF radio, and since it's July 4, all slips are filled; However, I remember some moorings just outside the marina. It's early afternoon when we secure to a mooring buoy. I head out in my dinghy to check into the marina office. Just as I am leaving, another dinghy is heading back, so I pull over to ask him if there's a place to tie up while checking in.

"Oh, no," he said. "You don't want to go in there with that. They don't like dinghies inside their marina."

"Okay, thanks," I reply. So, I enter the marina and tie up far away from the boat slips and walk to the office.

"Hello," I said. "I'm out on a mooring and want to pay for the overnight stay. (A mooring was $8 per night, so I gave him a brand new $20-dollar bill.)

"Sorry, I don't have change...."

"Well, keep the change," I said, "but can you tell me where I can tie my dinghy up so I can go ashore?" He politely pointed the way.

I return to the boat to pick up my friend, and we head to shore. At the beach, they have an excellent bar and restaurant, so we sit down at the bar to finally unwind. I have my one-drink limit and some great island food. After lunch, we head to the beach and later walk around and do a little shopping. Just after dark, we are back on the boat to watch their Fourth of July fireworks. I count one, maybe two reaching an altitude of about thirty feet!

The next morning, we must start the journey home with a stop at good old Albert's place. We make it safely through Whale Cay Channel and approach the marina, so I give my best friend a call on the marine radio.

"Albert, this is the sailing vessel APPARENT WIND looking for dockage for the night."

He replies with the same ol' message—he has "only one space left, reserved...blah, blah, blah," probably not realizing this was his wealthy American friend calling!

"Hey, Albert, go (I did use a swear word here) and that one dock space, up yours!" So, we end up anchoring off New Plymouth for the night.

It's still early, so we launch the dinghy and decide after our disastrous week—to finally enjoy some clear water by trying out my new snorkeling gear. Now I'm not exaggerating about this, but if I remember right, Mike takes at least fifteen minutes to get from the boat to the dinghy, and the boat even has a walk thru transom. The first step into an unstable dinghy usually causes this condition.

Finally, we motor out to an area that's good for snorkeling. I get my gear out, ready to jump in, and my brand new $50 diving mask falls apart. I just can't believe this! And my friend's brand new $50 mask barely fits over my left eye. So, we jump in - to at least feel the cool, clear water. We're attacked by a flock of birds. It just gets no better than this! Don't wait any longer. You should buy yourself that much sought after boat you've dreamed of and enjoy pleasure boating like the rest of us.

The next morning, I think, was a Friday. You see I never keep a log, so if I ever tried to get a job as a boat captain, they couldn't hold my trips against me.

Well, we head back along the bank the same way we came, trying to get Barometer Bob on the marine radio to check the latest weather report. If the weather showed favorably, I would leave the protected bank and head directly to Florida. No word from Bob, so we set course for Great Sale Cay but pass up anchoring and continue to West End. If the weather turns bad, I will tuck behind Mangrove Key: about 24 nautical miles in the direction we are heading.

It's now Saturday morning, and we have arrived at West End. The place is loaded with boats. So, we pull into the marina, and I notice a small space between boats at the fuel dock. I turn to Mike and tell him, "If anyone asks what we're doing here, just blame the author's writing style for our jumping in line." With the boat tied to the dock, a woman approaches and offers to help us.

"Hey, where do you go to get some fuel?" I ask.

"I can help," she says and has an attendant fuel us up. (See how all this creative stuff works?)

After topping off the fuel tank, we head out to anchor just off the western shore. This is where the fun really kicked in. With help from the boat's halyard line, we lift the dinghy we've been towing to secure her on the bow for the trip home. As my friend lowers the dinghy, the line slips through his hands. I now find myself under the dinghy, and I'm so tired I can't move it. (With a digital camera, I could've made a lot of money on this trip!)

After laughing for about an hour (5 minutes) we finally secure the dinghy to the bow, and I head for the comforts below to rest. Entering the cabin, I peek out the window and notice the sailboat next to mine must have left. I pop my head out and see a rather large water spout heading our way. The sailboat alongside us hadn't moved; we are dragging anchor and heading for the beach!

"Up!" I yell. "We got to go!" We haul in the anchor and head away from the spout and out to sea.

When leaving, I notice a few smaller sailboats following, but after the passing storm lifted, I see no other boats and the land is missing.

"Oh well, let's continue and head back to Florida." I am so tired I can't figure how much time I've been at the helm without rest.

I must have fallen asleep in the early morning only to wake to a rather large passenger vessel heading the same direction. How the ship missed us is anyone's guess, but a few hundred yards is way too close for comfort. I did have my radar alarm set, but it never sounded a warning, or maybe I just didn't hear it!

With the help from the fast-moving Gulf Stream, we find ourselves safely back at the fuel dock of one of my favorite marinas—on a Sunday morning. An employee approaches and asks if he can be of any assistance.

"Hello, I need to clear Customs, fuel up and secure a slip for my boat. I was here a few weeks back." He replies.

"Oh, NO, we can't help you, and if you stay on the fuel dock, I have to charge you by the hour while you wait for Customs!"

I look around, and the place is empty. "No slips?" I say to myself!

"Hey listen, I don't know what is wrong with this place, but how about you go (I also used bad language here) and that other guy that works here!" And depart we do.

Later in the day we pull into another marina for fuel and check slip availability there. They were most accommodating and find an excellent slip for my sailboat. Tied up and secured, we head to the restaurant on site for some much-needed food. While sitting there, I ask if there is taxi service, or if I could pay someone to drop us off in town so I can get my car that I left before the start of my trip.

"Sure," says a person sitting near us. "Here, take my car."

(I don't remember what I said or did, but I was shocked at this act of kindness.)

After an excellent meal, we head to get my car, which I had parked at a friend's condo for the past few weeks. I leave a thank-you note and even drop in fifty cents to show my gratitude—and to supplement her usual off-the-wall comments. Her husband was a close friend of mine, and we used to get in so much trouble when they had their boat docked in Sanford. He would buy so much computer stuff off eBay, and to everyone's amusement, had no idea what the hell he just bought. The stuff just showed up. He even had his own Federal Express truck and driver that came daily.

One day, his wife came home from the office, and we were sitting in the computer room. She looked around and noticed the closet doors were closed, and she knew they are never closed.

"OK, Honey…what did you buy now?" she asks. So, she opens the closet, and there are three large boxes containing computer monitors. Huge screens, by the way, HUGE!

"But, Honey, listen," he tells her, "I paid only $1 each for them!" Disgusted, she left.

"Hey, Buddy," I said. "You know you can't use these monitors."

"Why not?" he asked.

"You'll probably have to change your computer video card because the one that you have probably won't support that size." "So, Buddy, how much did you pay for them?"

"Only $1, but when she finds out how much I paid to have them shipped ... that worries me!"

Now back to the marina, I decide to keep the boat there until I can arrange to haul her back to Sanford. While at the dock, I mingle with the other sailors and ask one: "Hey, what's going on over at that other marina?"

"Oh, you don't want to go over there!"

"Oh, okay thanks. I just wished I had talked to you before I did go over there!"

My experience just pours out of my foul mouth with every swear word I can think of, encouraged by their sympathetic facial expressions.

So, I thought about keeping my boat at this marina so I could spend time here and take advantage of the beaches. But, boy, I was still mad at how I was treated at the start of my journey, and couldn't wait to talk to the marina manager. With the passing weeks, however, I forgot about the trip. One weekend when I was there I learned that some people were let go from the other marina where I had *fond* memories. Booyah! Life is good again.

CHAPTER 10
South America Delivery

A text that just said "Bumpy Ride" was all it took to get a reply from me that day in December. Years would go by between Captain Cub and me, but "Bumpy Ride" would always be our language for "Hello" and "When are we going?" For this trip, we were to take his vessel, the 105' Azimut, the BLUE HORIZON, from Palm Beach, Florida, to her new owners in South America. On our arrival in South America, Cub would take possession of their trade, an 82' Sunseeker. To make the trip, this journey would take us through the Bahamas, Turks & Caicos, and finally Jamaica, our last fueling stop before the final run to Colombia.

The four-man crew was Captain Cub, Captain Pedro, Captain Cole, and Yours Truly. Captain Cub's responsibility was to get us safely to Colombia and without yelling at me too much. Once there he was to turn this vessel over to a very wealthy and respected family. Their talented captain, Pedro, was along to assist and familiarize us with the workings of the vessel. But Pedro's real passion is his music. In Colombia, he is well known as "Pedro Rock."

This gifted singer and songwriter with his distinctive sound blends his Latin influences with rock music. Pedro has received several international awards, both in composition and in independent music promotion. Become a fan at www.reverbnation.com/pedrorockmusic.

Hey, Buddy! I'll send you a copy of my book if you send me your CD, *Lo Que Te Toca,* and throw in some Santander Chocolate-Covered Cacao Nibs?

Also aboard was Cole, a well-seasoned captain with experience throughout the Caribbean, Atlantic, and the Mediterranean. When you meet him, you'll find he's a very friendly person, and he sure can make you laugh, but aboard he is all business! Yep, we found our safety and entertainment officer. The show comes later in Colombia as he amuses, not just the crew, but everyone around him. And, then there's me, old and not seasoned but well overcooked. I swear I heard Cub say, "Get those old legs moving," while handling lines, at least, ten times during this trip!

Photograph by: Pedro Cordero
www.pedrorock.com

We left on a Monday at 10 p.m. from Palm Beach. This was the only route possible because of the cruising fuel limits of this vessel. This thirsty vessel was packing twin MTU diesel inboard engines at 2,000hp triple turbo each, and at a speed of 28 knots, she burns through 220 gallons per hour. Most of the trip we ran 16 knots at 120 gallons per hour. From Jamaica to South America, we ran 12 knots at 80 gallons per hour--the longest run, and to conserve fuel, if possible. The total trip was approximately 1,414 nautical miles, consumed over 10,600 gallons of fuel, and took 96 running hours. The longest run, Northern Jamaica to Cartagena was about 500 nautical miles and took 40 hours in 25-knot winds off the port bow. If you're looking for a Weight Loss Cruise, this is the one you want to make. I give it 5-Stars.

On my first night at sea and cruising at 16 knots, I must confess I was a little concerned about hitting something floating since we couldn't see anything in front of us. Here is where I was questioning myself on why I was there. Radar was good to have, but in rough conditions, you get way too many false echoes. This bothered me, but after the second night, I felt more comfortable at the helm, but I still worried. I froze the first two nights on the bridge and had brought only a windbreaker.

My good friend, Captain Bud, was kind enough to bring me down to Palm Beach from Sanford to drop me off. It was then I decided I didn't want to carry all my gear, so I left my full weather outfit in the car. Hey, I was heading south to some hot weather. What was I thinking? These were the things I could've used on this trip!

Now, if you ever get a chance to meet Buddy, you're in for a delightful experience. He helps everyone around the marina including me. Also, Bud and his lovely wife Mary often join Lynn and me while cruising on much bigger ships. That's the comfort and safety we enjoy, and Princess Cruises is the only way we go. We try to go a few times a year with the help of our knowledgeable Princess cruise planner, Nora, who also promises to buy my book!

The trip wasn't easy and included terrible working hours. On your typical rough water day, it took about an hour to reach the galley. We each ran 2-hour watches with 4-hours off and 2-hours standby, which meant you stayed in the pilothouse in the case of an emergency. I lost over 1-pound of weight daily, not the healthiest of weight loss programs.

The first stop was Highborne Cay in the Exumas about 60 nautical miles southeast of Nassau. We left the deep waters of the Tongue of the Ocean and made the shallow crossing of 40 nautical to the east to Highborne Cay in the late afternoon. We wanted to fuel and exit the shallow waters before sunset or we would've had to wait until morning.

The BLUE HORIZON held 4000 gallons of diesel, and it sure takes a few hours to top off. The sun was setting fast, but it looked like we would get out of there with an hour of daylight to spare.

Photograph by: John Lucarell
Bud & Mary

Not so fast! Those words will live with me forever. But for now, the marina doesn't take American Express and Captain Cub wanted to know if anyone had $9,000 in cash to pay the fuel bill. I started to look in my wallet like I had the money. What was I thinking!?

Now for some good news! Just before sunset, the Captain finally reached the vessel's corporate office, and things were settled over the phone. Our satellite phone did not work the entire trip, but we sure had DirecTV. That little guy inside the satellite-tracking dome was probably working overtime trying to keep us aligned with the satellite while we were bouncing about!

Out in time! The next stop was the Turks & Caicos and the end of our DirecTV signal. (Little dome guy will be so bored!) Let me think.... We left the Exumas about 6 p.m. and arrived for our second fuel stop the next day around 2 p.m. Even though we were a yacht in transit, we had to clear Customs before leaving the boat and fueling. This was my favorite run and the stars lit the skies and the seas before us. The evening sky so clear that you could reach up and almost touch a star. I found my calling that night: when I grow up, I want to be a Captain as courageous as ours. See, this is what you say if you want to stay on the right side of your captain!

The run to Blue Haven Marina in Provo, Turks, was about 315 nautical miles and what a beautiful area! Our primary task, besides fuel, was getting Dramamine for me. We arrived early afternoon, and after clearing Customs, the crew walked about to stretch their legs. I was the gasman and had to stay onboard and supervise the fueling in the case of spills. At least, I got to take pictures of the mega yachts in the marina.

"Cubby, I have a feeling we're not in Sanford anymore!"

We were all fueled, fed, and out to sea that day around 6 p.m. with Jamaica our next stop about 340 nautical miles to the south. This would be our last fuel stop before the long run to Colombia. A short time after leaving the Turks & Caicos, we had issues with our GPS navigational charts: that is, we had no GPS charts. We had an old paper chart from 1960 with water stains, coffee stains, missing pieces, blood stains (oh crap, those are mine, now I'm in trouble) and black spots that looked like swatted fly marks. This meant that, again, we had *ZERO* GPS guidance and had to rely on plotting our own course and waypoints.

Okay, I may have exaggerated a little about the chart.

So, Captain Cub says: "Plot me a course to Jamaica and Cartagena."

I had to ask him four times if he wanted me to do this: I was sick from school the day they covered chart plotting in 8-foot seas. The charts on hand were called small-scale charts—no harbor entrance details. It gets no better than this! With high winds, choppy seas, and no sleep we finally reach Port Antonio in the Northern part of Jamaica at the Eastern end. This is the part of the run where I questioned again why I was doing this.

Arriving in Jamaica around 4 p.m., we carefully maneuver the vessel towards the small inlet. Now remember: we have no charts. However, we have Cole's—cracked-screen—iPhone, in which the charts needed to find our way safely in are securely posted. (I know; don't you just love this!) With instructions from the marina, we proceed towards the service yard for fuel.

IT ONLY GETS FUNNIER

Three Customs agents show up a short time later, and Captain Pedro takes charge of the formalities. After I had said hello to the passing group; our captain asked if they would not mind removing their shoes before entering the boat, and from that moment, all went quiet. It's still quiet – The one agent said, "You want us to take off our shoes?"

"Yes," Pedro replied.

Then the big guy – yes, it's always the big guy – says: "There is no (the big guy used a swear word right after he said "no") way I'm going to take off my shoes!"

And that was the start of a stare down between our captain and the agents. By then I had assumed the position – hands up against the bulkhead with my legs spread! At least, the fuel attendant laughed! Finally, inside they all go, complete with shoes, and I was back at the fuel pump, which took only about three hours, but we couldn't depart until 10 p.m. We were waiting for the new vessel manager to arrive to make the trip from Jamaica to Colombia with us.

While we waited, Cub cooked the crew a fabulous meal of salad, potatoes, pasta and steak, which we surely needed before heading out again. A late departure was my concern on this dark, rainy, and windy night. Yep, we can't see much as we head out, and would run close to the reefs until we cleared the Eastern side of Jamaica.

It's Thursday. In inclement weather, we make our turn south to Cartagena, Colombia, our longest run. This section of the Caribbean winds always blows 25 knots or more. The BLUE HORIZON was equipped with stabilizers and with an easterly wind at our beam the vessel handled great. Oh, there were times at night you tried to find something you could hold on to, but fear had already left my body as a freighter, The GEORGIA T, was heading the same direction and flanked us all night with less than fifteen miles on the beam.

The BLUE HORIZON had the state of the art electronics installed before leaving for Colombia. The Automatic Identification System (AIS) is an automatic tracking system used on ships and by Vessel Traffic Services (VTS) for identifying and locating vessels by electronically exchanging data with other nearby ships. AIS information supplements marine radar, which continues to be the primary method of collision avoidance for water transport.

I had the perfect watch—5 a.m. to 7 a.m. when you witness the sunrise: no buildings, trees, traffic jams or standing in line for coffee. It's just you, and if you could make it to the galley that morning, you enjoyed your coffee. What an incredible feeling I get drinking that first cup up on the bridge in open seas. For the past 45 years, most of my boating was confined to the peaceful waters of the St. John River in Florida. But out on the big pond, you experience happiness and laughter, fear and terror - and usually all on the same day. Nothing like it! And every time I go to sea on a boat delivery, I want more. If only I could only get my daughter's permission!

Photograph by: John Lucarell
Captains Cub and Pedro

It's Saturday morning, and Cartagena is in sight after two nights at sea. The trip is almost over, and the laughter and childish behavior come out in all of us.

{Kevin} I think Cole is right.
{Pedro} Who's Cole?

{Kevin} He's the other guy on this trip with us!
{Incoherent} chatter and laughter
{Kevin} See, this little dot on the screen must be us, and this shaded area must be Cartagena.
{Pedro} We're in Cartagena already?
{Kevin} Look, this dot is us. Oh Crap, now there are two dots!

CHAPTER 11

Cartagena, Colombia

Cub wants to bring me up to speed once we enter Colombia. Something tells me I should be a little concerned.

We enter the main shipping channel around 1 p.m. and proceed through the harbor to a marina off Manga to clear Customs. Other than a cruise ship in port, we are the new big *lady* coming to town to make the many onlookers "Oooh" and "Aaah." Before we secured the last line over, about twenty crew from the new vessel owners board us and immediately start to clean and organize the boat.

Okay, now what? Captain Pedro was informed the boat must be readied and back out to sea by sunset. Yes, five hard days and nights to get this boat here and back out again on a charter. "Oh, joy!" was heard among the fearless!

So, the new crew is everywhere cleaning, polishing and rearranging our scattered furniture. I hear someone shout (in English more or less),

"Whose Tootsie Roll Pops are these? They're scattered all over the place. Why should I have to clean this mess up!"

I don't say a word! Cub, Cole and I just stay out of their way at the salon table until the entertainment director for this company shows up. He reminds me of Don Vito Corleone portrayed by Marlon Brando in *The Godfather* film.

At that exact moment, Cub turns and says: "Whatever he offers you, please do not turn him down; it is a sign of disrespect!"

"Offer me what? Like an offer I can't refuse?" I ask.

"Dude – you're in Colombia and prostitution is legal here," Cub replies.

Wow, here comes that uncomfortable feeling I usually get in situations like this! And as Don Vito is approaching our table, sweat is pouring from my body.

"Cub, don't be doing this to me; I'm not interested in what he's about to say, and this is not what you're not paying me for." (That's right. I wasn't getting paid for this trip. Besides, I'm aboard just for everyone's amusement.)

"Now listen," Cub says, "if they offer you someone for the evening, please don't refuse!"

"Okay," I reply. "How about I just take her to the movies?"

"Something just like that," Cub said, "but try and be less pusillanimous."

"Okay," I reply. "But listen to me! I don't understand the language. I can barely understand you, and now of all times you start using big words? "Oh no, here comes Don Vito......"

"Now youz geys wanta anyting to eats?" he asks. Youz lik chikin? I send out fer chikin; I know youz geys goin to like our chikin." (To authenticate the story, in reality, this person was pleasant and spoke excellent English, probably better than mine; looked nothing like the Godfather. But when you make up a story and words like I just did, you must admit it sounds funnier and scarier: like an old gangster movie! I hope he doesn't read this; he will spot that run-on-sentence immediately – I mean no disrespect!)

The food is delivered and, yes, Don Vito sits with us. I want to leave before any further offerings are announced. Damn, he's speaking before I can get away.

"Now youz geys, we take yuz to our hoetels. Ands - If youz wanta some food youz sign – If youz wanta some drink yuz sign – youz wanta some girls – youz – ah - No sign - I bring. Better yet I take youz to hookers' bar."

I can't believe this is happening, but if I were taller with money, this could be a fun city to hang out in. But, I am so out of my element; the country, culture, and the language barrier just overwhelm me.

Well, it's time to pack our belongings and head for the launch alongside to take us to the hotel. Now some would imagine this launch would be like a dinghy or small craft. Oh no! How about a 28' go fast

Sportfish with twin 300hp outboards. I don't have enough time to even hold on as he juices this puppy. Now, from the boat dock to the city pier by the hotel is about one nautical mile away. We made it there in 52 seconds! I thought the language difficulty was enough of an issue; when we docked, my body hadn't arrived yet!

From the boat dock, we walk a few blocks to the hotel right on the beach. You would've thought you were at South Beach in Miami. The locals even call this South Beach. After we check in, Cub, Cole, and I head for the bar. One thing I remember Cub telling me is that when Cole is on the boat, he's all business, but off it's a different story. "Whatever you do, for your own safety," he warns, "don't go anywhere with him. Trust me, he doesn't slow down, and you're much too old to keep up."

At that exact moment of memory recall Cole turns and says: "Hey look, if Veto Corleone doesn't show, how about we head down to the hookers' bar?"

"Look. I'm exhausted, and Cub is probably right, I'm much too old. How do you do this? Aren't you tired after this trip?" He pulls up his shirt and exposes his own bandolier loaded with 5-hour ENERGY drinks!

Okay, let me bring you up to speed – I'm out of my element; I don't understand the language; I'm tired, some say old, and sitting next to a non-stop partier.

I say, "You know, guys, I have had an eventful trip. I'm tired, and all I want to do is sleep and in the morning, have a nice sit down non-moving type of breakfast." And off I go to my well-stocked room, and, that bed sure felt good!

The next morning around six, I get a call from Cub, saying "Meet you in ten. We have to go and move the 82 Sunseeker next to the 105 Azimut so all parties can transfer their personal items and gear."

"What, no breakfast?" I reply. And when you say it in a low tearful voice the Cub caves in, and I finally get to sit down and have food that's not moving – so I think. The only thing I could recognize was the orange juice and never knew those were eggs. So much for breakfast!

Off we go on that slow-boat-to-China that got us to the marina before I got my other foot in. We untie the 82, motor over to the 105, and moor the boats together. Quickly, all is done, and we head back to secure the 82 to her dock. Cub tells me the new owners want him to go with Captain Pedro to help in case of any issues with the boat, so he'll be gone for a few days, but he's leaving someone to translate for me while I'm in Cartagena. So, my translator and I return to the hotel for some rest and relaxation—unless I run into Cole.

While I'm here in Cartagena, and I have the day off, why not see the city? I have my own interpreter. I call Cub's attentive driver, Hernando, who runs a local tour business and speaks English. My confidence is rising; I'm back in the flow. And, I don't need no stinking help! (In just a few chapters, I will regret ever saying that!)

Photographed by: Hernando Torres Durante
http://www.cartagenasunrisehomeboys.com

So, Hernando shows and off we go on his informative tour, zipping along cobblestone streets bordered by lovely, colorful colonial style buildings. Cartagena's character and its 16th-century plazas, vendors, and street art are in two picturesque neighborhoods: the walled Old Town and the rising Barrio Getsemani. I also notice that no one stops for pedestrians, so walkers become fair game.

We visit the highest point in Cartagena, the convent Convento de la Popa, which has in its chapel an image of La Virgen de la Candelaria, the patroness of the city. The convent's name literally means the Convent of the Stern and was founded by the Augustine fathers in 1607. Its official name is Convento de Nuestra Señora de la Candelaria. The views from here are beautiful; you can see all over the city.

On our way, back we stop at the Castillo De San Felipe De Barajas. Hernando tells me this fort was built back in the 17th century for the city's fortification and had an excellent strategic location. We finally make our way back to our hotel sometime late afternoon and meet up with Cole, who is still going strong in the hotel bar. Late afternoon becomes early evening, and we're still at Cole's favorite place. He comments on the lame rum and coke drink I've been sipping the last few hours and says, "You know what? I know a place if you want an excellent rum drink." One good thing about this rum drink place is that it's only about 50 feet away on the beach. The only thing merciless about getting there is you must cross the street. Do you recall my mentioning walking a few paragraphs back? Safely crossing the street sober requires all bodily functions working properly. I honestly don't remember ever crossing the street.

But I find myself safely parked on a bar stool, holding on so I won't fall, and watching a man prepare my huge coconut rum knockout punch! I also remember that while I'm waiting, a woman walks up from behind, and I feel her hands all over me.

"No – No!" I reply. "Un memento and please stop!"

Well, she is on the beach offering massages to beachgoers who are under the influence of alcohol. I'm certain that this is not going to help my situation. Meanwhile, Cole is sitting here laughing and taking pictures: "Oh," he proudly says; "I got this." And he paid for the service. The next thing I know, my clothes come off, cameras are a-clicking, and I am getting the rub-down. Honestly, I would have to see Cole's pictures to see if I was sitting there naked.

Now, how I got back to the hotel bar across the street and fully clothed is anyone's guess. But we're sitting there, and Cole's outgoing personality takes over the crowd. All that I can vouch for is that his last night in Colombia was "Epic."

The rest of my night went something like this: I'm in my room over by the sink for obvious reasons and notice a fancy card. One item on it says something in Spanish, like *"tratamiento de belleza,"* a beauty treatment, which could be yours for an amount in pesos. I crawl to the bed and check the app on my phone to see how much in USD. Then I crawl back and check the second item. The last thing got my attention: For "Marque 1 condones," and then I passed out!

The next morning Hernando picked me up to take me to the airport. While in route, I asked, "Hey, Hernando, if I come back, where would you recommend I stay?"

He then turned and replied, "You want one, two, three-bedroom condo on the beach? I take care of this for you. When you arrive at the airport, I pick you up, and if you want to eat my house, my wife a great cook, and we hang out."

So, we reached the airport. No handshakes, but man hugs—I had found another great friend for life. We text and talk back and forth every week to just say hello. Hernando also helped Captain Cub move the 82 Sunseeker from Colombia to Panama, where I was to join up later and help bring her back to Ft. Lauderdale. So, if you are ever in Colombia and feeling lost as I was, and in need of a friend, Hernando is his name, born and raised in Cartagena!

I'm at the airport and checking my luggage and answering a hundred questions at the ticket counter. I then proceed to Airport Security, and I am thankful to be the only one in line. The officer speaks Spanish, and here I am frozen in time and can't talk. This is the last man to keep me from getting home, and nothing I say is helping my cause. The officer knows a few English words, just enough to let me pass. I'm now comfortably sitting at the gate waiting for my flight when Hernando starts texting me through an internet phone app, with all the services he has to offer until we finally say goodbye.

Did you know that any pictures sent through "WhatsApp" are automatically saved in your picture folder on your phone? I didn't know that! But, I did keep the lovely picture of the two-bedroom condo on the beach he sent!

CHAPTER 12
Long Day Ahead

In January, I got a call from Cub saying that the vessel's owner wanted his 82' Sunseeker brought to Ft. Lauderdale and Cub wanted to see if I was recovered from the last trip.

"Absolutely," I replied, not knowing what I'd agreed to! During the next few weeks, I researched Bocas Del Toro, Panama, the area the boat was docked. On the Internet, it looked like another Trip of a Lifetime. You see, everything you read in this book and on the Internet must be true!

A few days before I'm to depart for Panama, Cub calls to inform me I would have to bring a much-needed 300-gallon bladder fuel tank on the flight with me. Without this extra portable fuel tank, this vessel did not have the cruising range between stops unless you want to travel at 5 knots. Now, as if I'm not already freaking out about just getting there by myself, let alone carrying boat parts, this new layer of responsibility complicates things even further. For one thing, I did not know the Panamanian Customs laws. All I had known from the Cub was that this February, he "would need help to move the boat that's in an isolated part of Panama…It should take only four airports, two airlines, one puddle jumper, one taxi, maybe a bus, one water taxi, and a four-mile hike to get there." The Cub, always the kidder!

Initially, this 82' Sunseeker trade-in from Colombia would just make the short trip to Panama. From there the owner wanted to cruise around and explore the islands and then head to Colon, Panama. At that point, the boat would be loaded on a container ship and hauled back to the States because of the cruising fuel limits of this vessel. Apparently, a change in plans (and a book in the making!)

So, here are my first two problems:

1) How am I going to carry and drag this probably huge box containing the bladder tank, weighing sixty pounds with my bad back through the airport and pass it off as baggage?
2) It's Sunday, and I'm scheduled to leave on Monday from Orlando International Airport; this package is still in Ft. Lauderdale, and I'm at work. I have no idea what I'm up against.

Do you remember Bud from a few chapters back? He saves the day and satisfies my curiosity by driving to get this package for me. When he returns several hours later, we unpack the tank to see what my options would be. To you and me, this looks like a folded-up vinyl tarp. But, just to us. The Panamanian Customs office likely has a different opinion. They'll probably wonder, "How much coffee can these idiots cram into this container?" and "Why here, and not Colombia, where they actually have the best coffee?" I am certain that the Panamanian officials received a countrywide broadcast memo to BE ON THE LOOKOUT FOR ANY SUSPICIOUS-ODD-LOOKING CHARACTERS ARRIVING IN THE COUNTRY! Yes, that would be me!

So, Bud and I try to see if this 60-pound item would fit into a large suitcase I had. With just a few jumps up and down with my weight on it, we finally close the top enough to zip it up. Hopefully, I won't have to unzip this thing until safely aboard the boat. (I was wrong with that thought!)

Monday morning arrives, I'm up at 2 a.m., finished packing and waiting for Bud to pick me up at 3 a.m. for the drive to Orlando to catch my early morning flight. The trip is good, and in three hours I'm safely on the ground. (This, however, will not always be the case.) I arrive in Panama on a Monday at 10 a.m., and already I'm in my bad dream. I cannot find any signs that say "Baggage." You would think I could find someone that speaks some sort of English! No! Not until I finally spot a flight attendant and ask her help:

"Sir, you go down this corridor and go right at the end, but don't go left."

A short time later I find myself at the end of the hallway where I see plenty of lefts, but not one right.

Again, I seek help. "Can you please help me?"

"Okay, you go down that corridor, and I think you make a left."

(I say to myself, "Okay, no need to panic. Gather your thoughts. Remember you haven't even made it to Customs yet!") So, I walk back towards the gate where I finally notice a small sign that says "Baggage" one floor down, and I'm saved for the moment!

After standing in a long line, I pass through Immigration looking for my luggage. Now this is where all hell breaks loose—when Customs has me open my luggage. As I unzip the case, the agent gets a good look at what I'm carrying, and I get that feeling: This will not end well. The officer looks down at my luggage; she then looks up to see my reaction. I was cool as a cucumber. She looks down again, and up again. I was about to make a smart-ass remark when she replies in a scary Panamanian self-possessed female voice these words that will haunt me for as long as I live, "*Yuz com wid me!*"

Well off to Luggage Jail I go. I probably match the countrywide broadcast memo to be on the lookout for any suspicious-odd-looking character arriving in their country, or they have never seen a boat part like the one I'm carrying. Just in case, I had all the documents with me and, to you and me, it still looked like a folded vinyl tarp.

Now, you would think that among at least 10 agents who deal with international travelers, one would speak English. And, if you believe that three of the same alphabet letters is just a recurring social event, try "TTT" on for comfort! The "Teeter Totter Taunting" begins. That cool-as-a-cucumber guy a few minutes' back is now an old dried up 63-year-old prune. Back and forth I go, trying to find out what's going on. Then--here she is--staring at me like she adores old prunes or something.

"You look like you could use some help," she offers.

I think I'm saved! I just want to drop to my knees and beg forgiveness for ever knowing Captain Cub! (Well, it didn't happen quite that way.) She offers to translate for me. I now feel a little more in control of the situation, but just a little. (Okay, it may have happened that way! The part about dropping to my knees and begging for forgiveness!)

So back and forth we go with the Customs Officials until I finally find out what they want. My interpreter tells me I must find my driver who is taking me to the other airport where I'm to take my flight to Bocas Del Toro. She hands me a piece of paper with words all in Spanish.

"Okay," I tell her, "I know a few of the words like name, make of car, license plate, but what is this sentence?"

She says: "Ask if your driver is seeing anyone. You know... Is he single?"

"They can't be serious!" I said.

"No, that's for me," she replied. "You see, when I was walking out in the terminal, I saw a handsome man holding up a sign "Desperate American." I just figured he was here for you and why not take advantage of the situation you happen to be in." (Okay, I just made that up, but I had you going there for a minute!)

Seriously, she tells me to "Go through those doors, find your driver and get the information. You can return over at those doors, and they will let you back in."

Now, I'm out in the terminal, and I can't believe all the people holding up signs waiting for their passengers. Oh, look! There's one that says "Prison Tours" and another saying "Ride Me All Day." I'm in a panic trying to find my driver who I made arrangements with before leaving Florida. About 15 minutes later, I find him holding up the sign: yep, "Desperate American"! I'm most fortunate that he speaks English. So, I tell him what's happening, apologize for the delays, and assure him that I will take care of any additional fees. Once the driver hands me the information, I walk back to the Customs area. Nope - can't get back in, and instructed to get a pass. Now, I must go three flights up and stand in another line—like at an amusement park to get a badge—and surrender my passport. A few minutes later I'm back in Customs Luggage Jail, sitting again, and no one is talking to me.

Frustrated and mad, I undo the rubber band (this is creative writing at work) from the doorknob I thought they were using to keep me in the luggage room the size of a closet. Looking all around, I'm careful not to make any sudden moves as I untie the knot, using the skills I gained from Brian's knots back at our marina. Once freed, I wander outside the office and see the lovely woman who helped me earlier.

"You're still here!" she asked.

"Listen," I explain. "I gave customs the information, but nothing is happening, and I'm worried about missing my flight at the other airport."

"Let me go check for you."

She returns to tell me that I must pay for a Customs agent to travel with me while in Panama and did I get the name of my handsome driver? Yep, just like Cub – always the kidder!

I'm now standing in yet another line, waiting my turn to pay the fees. My frustration grows because I don't want to miss my flight. The teller finally finishes the online form I need to leave the airport. Now paid and feeling less like a wealthy American, I grab my baggage and leave Customs. But, I hit another snag on my way out: they want their rubber band back! The good news, if any, is that once they hand me off to the agents at Albrook Airport, I should be okay for the rest of my trip. When leaving, I hear: "Enjoy your stay here in Panama!"

CHAPTER 13
Same Day—How's that Possible?

With my driver and Customs agent in tow, the criminal from Florida heads up to retrieve his passport, and there she is again: the lovely helpful lady says, "You should have paid more attention in your Spanish Class, and how's Steve doing these days?"

(Just like Cub – always the kidder!) She wanted to know if all was okay. I told her I couldn't thank her enough for all her help or I'd probably still be sitting there even after my book is written.

"By the way," I said, "I do apologize. My name is Luke."

"Hi, I'm Maria..." and hands me her card. "If you need any other help while in Panama, here's my number; please don't hesitate to call." I look down at her business card and see that she is a medical doctor.

I said, "Maria, I'll probably need a doctor before the day's over." And with parting smiles, we say goodbye.

So, I'm off to the Albrook Airport for my 45-minute ride and Freedom Bus Tour and for an extra fee I could take advantage of the Prison Tour. I decide to save the excursion for the next time I'm in town. I arrive at the airport just in time to catch my flight and deposit more money into the local economy. From here, I would board the last flight to Bocas Del Tora and, hopefully, start to enjoy my time in Panama. Nope, this is where it starts all over again, and the continuing fees and small print in Spanish kick in.

It is now 2 p.m., and you know what? I have no idea what time it is, but I find myself standing comfortably at the airport. You see, there are only a few chairs in this entire place. Okay, I may be fibbing some; I saw a one-seat bench, at the entrance, also a small coffee shop and three tables near a refreshment center. So, I'm standing, my luggage is being held again by Customs, and I can't understand a single word being said. About 30 minutes later, an agent takes me up to a second-floor office where I stand and wait more (like standing in line at an amusement park, but the park is closed, and you're the only one left). A few minutes later, an agent brings me a small chair, and there I sit in the middle of the room. Still no word on what's going on. Yep, no one speaks English. But, Hey, I'm in their country; this is their language, and I respect that. I should have studied a little Spanish!

About 15 minutes later, another agent takes me down to the ticket line where I can do more standing and more waiting for the agent who can talk to someone who speaks English. Now, I'm up that creek without a paddle whining, "My back is hurting, and my bad knee is giving me a fit." By the way, I've been walking with a limp since arriving at this airport.

While standing next to an Information Booth, a man behind the counter says, "Looks like you're having a bad day?"

Thinking I'm saved again, I replied, "Does it show?"

"I would like to help you," he says, "but the agent wants you to talk to that man behind the airline ticket counter."

So, after standing in another line, we reach the counter, and the back-and-forth translation begins. I am informed that now I must pay for a second agent to fly with me to Bocas Del Toro, and I also must pay for his airline ticket to and from. Oh, and my flight originally scheduled to depart at 4:15 p.m. is delayed by 3 hours.

It is now about 3:20 p.m. and the airline ticket translator points to the second-floor office where I am to pay the agent's fee for traveling with me while I'm in Panama. The last time I checked, I was still at the airport, but now feels like I'm slowly inching myself closer to the marina (hallucinating!). My translator tells me to go pay at 4:00 p.m.—Not at 3:45 p.m., but only at 4:00 p.m. I look down to check my watch: it doesn't even know what time it is! My instructions were clear: once I pay, I am to meet the agent going with me at the same spot where I was standing at 3:20 p.m. - at 4:45 p.m. - no earlier and no later - to purchase the additional airfare for the Customs Agent. Huh?

I need to get ahold of Cub, but the Internet signal is weak. So, with limited Internet access, I finally send a coded phone app smoke signal that I'd be late: leaving here at 7:15 p.m., and he better not leave me here in Panama!

"No worries, I'll be there!" he replies.

Soon after contacting the boat, I head for the refreshment center where I meet a guy from England. (How could I tell he was from England or from someplace other than here? Always look for someone with blonde hair!) We chatted some while waiting - You know the usual talk among fellow world travelers like, "Why do guys always over pack on trips?"

Also, "What do I think about the Effect of Snow on Plants and Their Interactions with Herbivores?" from an article by Mikeala Torp he'd read. I was stumped! You see, I'm from Florida and haven't seen snow since Chapter One!

I now found myself pacing back and forth wishing I had a response to his snow question. Not paying attention, I accidently wore off the mark left on the floor where I was supposed to be at 4:45 p.m. Hey, will someone please put me out of my misery! It is now 3:45, and I start my ascent to the top floor, bravely willing to risk bodily harm for disobeying their demand I go through that door at 4 p.m. and 4 p.m. only. As I was walking up those steps, I was telling myself that no way was I going to put up with this anymore, and I'll go through that door when I'm damn ready.

Oh, look! It's 4 o'clock, and the friendly Customs clerk takes more of my money. (How I accomplished this transaction in Spanish I'll never know.) Now I have receipt and proof I was in Panama! With that checked off my To-Do list, I begin my descent. (Do you like I used "ascent" and "descent" to prepare you for my airplane ride?)

Now with the airline tickets paid, I just can't wait to board and get the hell out of here! But, once you pay, you don't go to your gate because they have no assigned gate. So, you stand in line, but now the park is OPEN, and you're at the Magic Kingdom and waiting your turn to ride Big Thunder Mountain Railroad! But once the security doors open, they have a rather nice waiting room area with Internet access to everyone but me. Why am I the only one having Internet problems? Well, let me explain.

Before I left for Orlando, I decided to take my spare phone battery pack. The last time I traveled, all the communicating drained my battery. I thought this would help. I even copied all the phone numbers I would need on a piece of paper just in case I lost my phone. Unfortunately, the spare battery pack somehow shorted out (or something like that) and crashed my phone while all of this was happening in Panama. To this day, I have yet to locate that piece of paper with all those numbers! If any of my twelve friends ever get a phone call from someone named Rogelio Tacoma Salviano, that's probably because of me!

So, now we're not leaving at 7:15 p.m. like I was informed but 6:20 p.m. I don't see the agent and the announcements are in Spanish. The boarding pass is also in Spanish, and the only thing I can make out is my seat number 8C.

"Is this the flight to Bocas?" I ask.

I get nothing but smiles because they probably think they have all my money but don't want to appear rude! I'm finally on the plane, now looking for 8C. Someone is sitting there. Holy crap! I am on the wrong flight. My anxiety kicks in, and I turn to leave when I see the agent boarding, and I breathe again. (The breathing part is short lived!)

I'm told, "Just sit anywhere." I ready myself now for the takeoff. As we barrel down the runway, one of the prop engines stops. My anxiety level kicks to a new area of terror with some strange side effects explained a little later in the chapter! I never knew a plane could make all those noises. One of the English-speaking passengers said the pilot went down the wrong runway! I don't know what happened. Maybe they received a call from the international airport that the rubber band I returned was a forgery, and they're looking for me again. Maybe something happened mechanically because the last time I looked on Google Earth, there was only one runway. I was beginning to have that feeling I may never make it home! I just wished I were making this up at this point! So, the pilot turns the plane around to go back, and he tries the take off all over again. Finally, holding my breath—hey, look we're off the ground. But, I'm not sure I'm happy!

I can't wait for this day to be over. It's 6:45 p.m., or thereabout, and we should arrive around 7:30 p.m. You know what? I have no idea when this plane will land. All I know is that Cub said he would meet me at the airport, and I can't wait to see him and tell him how much I love traveling, the excitement and meeting new friends whose names I can't pronounce!

Now safely on the ground, my Customs agent passes me off to another agent at the Bocas del Toro airport. I'm now told the paperwork is "NOT IN ORDER," and again I'm being held, but now I'm an almost half-day well-seasoned world traveler. At least one person in the same room can translate for me.

I politely ask: "Tell me this, how can my documents be in order at the International Airport and in order at Albrook Airport, but when I get to you, they're not in order?" The translator tells me I'm missing a document.

"Look," I said, "the captain of the boat should be outside waiting for me. Can you please go out to the lobby and get him? I'm sure he has everything you need."

So, they go outside, and I hear them yell his name. They return and announce, "No, heze no here in elporte." Sweat is pouring off my body like Niagara Falls! A few minutes later the agent hands me a towel and with another person walks me through this small airport. I now stand outside in a dark, unpaved lot with no sign of Cub. Back and forth in a non-understandable dialog, I point to the airport door: "Look, I'm going back inside to wait for my Captain."

"No, wheeze closi elporte!" It's Panic Time-Again!

The Customs agent then hops on his bicycle and takes off, and I'm left standing with someone that I have no idea who he is? He stands about seven feet tall, and when you're as terrified as I am, everything around just looks big! But for the authenticity of the story, I'll put his height at six feet, four inches tall! So, he takes one of my bags and leads us towards town two miles away. Okay, it's only about a half a mile (but you must admit two miles sounded better, and I was hoping my readers—at this point—would be feeling my suffering. You can't make this stuff up; trust me, I've tried!)

He turns down an alley darker than the darkest street. "Believe you me," I'm thinking, "This is where they will find my body with my stained underwear from the airplane ride." I have a ton of cash (all legal and enough left to purchase coffee while here) strapped to my chest for boat operating expenses to make it back home! I have never been so scared or screwed in all my life. BUT, I haven't met the pirates yet, or drunk at Herby's in Roatan or Two Decks Up. But, I can't forget Teds, Way Outback, Jim's and Holy Toledo's in Mexico and boy, I sure made a fool of myself in Key West!

So, returning to my present problem, I slow my pace and look all around for someone to jump out from the bushes or from behind a building. What, exactly, was I capable of doing to defend myself? Look, I can't even take a fish off the hook. (Yours truly, "The Duct Tape Ninja," is having his own problems with pirates in Chapter Fifteen.)

Still alive, we finally make it to town and find some English speakers. They offer to give us a ride in a skiff to Isla Bastimentos, the island where the vessel is docked for $20. I also had to pay for the bicycle agent traveling with me. Boy, I didn't see that one coming!

I board just as Cub shows in a skiff from the marina. (Immediately after seeing him and, to add suspense to the movie script, I try desperately to grab the gun from the Customs agent and with my lightning reflexes and little resistance from him, I hold his weapon at point blank range to my head!)

Nope, all's good with Cub; I have no hard feelings about my day and what he put me through. I'm finally safe! I would go as far as hugging and kissing Cub. But he would try desperately to grab that same gun and place it at point blank range also at my head! (See, when you need additional word count for your book, you write material like that.)

In about twenty minutes, I'm aboard the vessel at the marina around who knows what time of night. The Customs agent is also on our boat; he gives Cub more troubling arguments about our paperwork not being complete. Luckily our other crew, Emanuel, is aboard and speaks Spanish. The agent also informs us that his office is closed so he must charge us additional fees until we can hand him what he needs back at his office the next day! All this while taking pictures of our illegal coffee container cleverly disguised as a bladder fuel tank.

Cub explodes – "By whose authority!" (I'm leaving out all the swear words that would've pushed my total word count by at least another fifty, maybe sixty, words.) That barrage of words isn't directed at me, but I'm shaking so much I set off the boat's alarm system! (... another lie.)

"Let me ask you this," says Cub, "what will it take for you to just go away?" When the agent does that famous Johnny Manziel's "show me the money" finger wiggle, our day is finally over! (More lies.)

Well, of course, he didn't do that; he was very friendly and helpful, and this was all cleared up the next day. No shots are fired, or finger gestures, only a light barrage of obscene language between the parties. And, by the time the dust had settled and the tiny red frogs from Red Frog Beach were asleep, the agent was even willing to pull my poster off the "suspicious odd-looking character" list!

CHAPTER 14

Bocas Del Toro, Panama

Bocas Del Toro, Panama to San Andres, Colombia
Departed Wednesday at 0730 - Arrived San Andres at 1730

Bocas Del Tora – Ah, what can I say other than I was glad to finally get there. With the tour of the Panamanian Customs arrival and procedures division a thing of the past, for now, I tell Cub I sure could use a drink and some food of which I had none all day. So off to Two Decks Up for refreshments and memory-making/sharing—Cub introduces me to the cook, Francisco from Costa Rica, and the two bartenders working that evening: Savannah from Brooklyn and Brooklyn from the Savannah (I was a little confused myself) up on the second deck.

It wasn't long after the drinks were going down easy and, for myself, it took little alcohol to put me away for good and make a fool (not a lie) of myself. I can always tell when I've had enough; it's when I have to go to the bathroom every two minutes and drinks are still being delivered there because I can't find my way back to the bar! But in the meantime, I sure loved the drinks Savannah was preparing, and I was always asking her for more ice. Cub knew exactly why I was doing this, and it didn't take long for Savannah to catch on either. The ice chest was on the floor across from me. Savannah had to turn away and bend over every time she went for ice. The tease was on. Just about then, my hamburger showed up, and the twerking, involving thrusting hip movements was a sight to behold! Or, so I was told!

I remember little after that, but when I finally woke the next morning, Cub was lying face down on the salon floor; my head was just inside with the glass door up against my neck and the rest of my body was lagging behind on the aft deck. After shaking off the alcohol influence to my body and stumbling about, I found Emanuel asleep in the engine room. I can't even explain that one!

We must have been watching *Mission Impossible- Rogue Nation* because the movie was still playing. I had to step over Cub to turn off the TV set, but I was careful not to disturb him or suffer the consequences like in the other Chapters. I just refer to it as Cub's "Recurring Limb Movement Cataclysmic Upsurge Disorder."

With everyone up and moving, the smell of just brewed coffee was a welcoming relief from last night expedition tour. About an hour later, Emanuel takes me to a restaurant on the beach just a short walk away for breakfast then a little sightseeing. He was trying to find a red frog along the way. These red frogs are the size of your fingernail: no such luck finding one. "We can climb this hill, and we should see some at the top," Emanuel suggested, but I was in no shape to climb that morning. The restaurant was on the beach and overlooked a beautiful setting for enjoying the sea breeze while having coffee. At Red Frog, there are multiple hiking trails, snorkeling spots, hidden beaches, cave systems, and a zip line canopy tour.

Later, back at the boat, we made modifications to secure our illegal coffee container cleverly disguised as a bladder fuel tank to the aft deck and clean my bloodstains off the heavy glass sliding doors. Okay, Cub secured the tank. I could barely stand and watch, so I just wandered off to explore on my own. I continued to check this impressive boat. I was looking forward to kicking back on what seemed like a comfortable lower station all electrically controlled captain chairs. I also was glad that the galley was nearby, and the navigation system was equally impressive with its massive number of unlabeled switches. Not just at the helm, switches were everywhere: at least thirty just in the main salon.

A little later, I found myself exploring the docks like all guys that work at a marina do. I checked out the dock construction and the floatation material used, their cleat placement pattern, how wide the main piers were, the water system and hose connections. Did the electrical pedestals use 120/240V via the 14 kV single-phase network or a variation of the 240 V Delta 4-wire system? And was their wifi system just as bad as ours?.

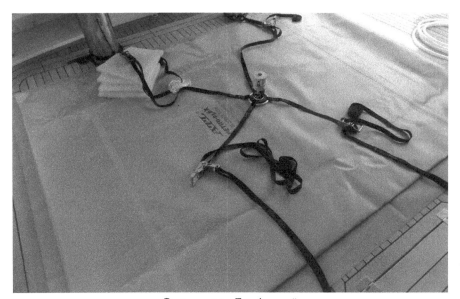

Photograph by: John Lucarell
300-gallon bladder fuel tank

After my two-minute fact-finding (And, their wifi was not as bad as ours) exploration, I talked with some locals. I learned that within the province of Bocas Del Toro, exists a broad range of habitats including lagoons, mangroves, estuaries, and coral reefs. They all serve as resources for food, migration, and nesting for the Leatherback, Hawksbill, and Loggerhead turtles. Isla Bastimentos is an excellent location to see the great abundance of Panama's birds. The tropical environment makes Bocas del Toro comparable to islands in the South Pacific. It's surrounded by lush green forest with very clear blue water.

Now, for us to leave Panama, we had to go into town and clear Customs; however, with the help of the Marina Manager's assistance. We loaded up in his center console and, with no slowing down on the choppy waters, we pounded back to town, Bocas Del Toro—my bad back and all and don't forget my bad knee. From there we made a left and walked to the southern end of Calle 3a Street, then to the Port Captain where Cub stopped to complete the required *Zarpe* (our Cruising Permit). The Captain's office was in a little box container right on the edge of the rugged street.

The rest of us headed due north to the government building 323 smoots away. (I looked up *smoot* in the dictionary and found it indicated a nonstandard, humorous unit of length, which I now use for reference. It was created as a fraternity prank and named after Oliver R. Smoot. In October 1958, he lay down repeatedly on a bridge so his fellow brothers could use his height of 5' 7" to measure the length.

A short time later, we arrived at the government building to clear Immigration and Customs - a simple, pleasurable and standard customary procedure. It was there we met the Immigrations officer, who spoke English and was a very pleasant person – until he met Emanuel. Emanuel's visa had expired, and now he was facing a severe penalty. So back and forth they went, trying to come to a reasonable settlement so Emanuel could leave the country with us. This probably took about an hour and then, it was my turn.

"Ah, Señor John, I see you came in by plane, said the agent. If you come in by plane and leave by plane, you need no visa. If you come in by plane and leave by car or bus, you need no visa. If you come in by boat and leave by boat, you need no visa. BUT, Señor John – you come in by plane, and you leave by boat – Ah, Señor John, you need a visa!"

"Sir," I said, "I wasn't expecting anything less! "So how much jail time am I looking at?"

"Ah, Señor John, no jail time; just $105 cash for a visa so you can stay and enjoy Panama for the next few months!"

"What if I'm only staying a day?" I asked.

"Ah, Señor John, so you're that funny American they warned me about from the airport that helped close down the bar last night. But, it's still $105!"

I paid for my visa, and we said our goodbyes and headed out to find Cub so we could clear Customs, the final hurdle to allow us safe passage out of Panama. As soon as we walked out of the building, Cub arrived but had made no progress in finding the Customs agent. (As in the movie script, maybe he didn't leave the boat alive last night? The plot thickens.) Kevin was told that the agent might be back today or sometime tomorrow. Cub's anger hovered about him, so we looked to find a place for lunch. Soon after that, we returned to Customs and, to our luck the agent was in his office—late, but In. He must have had a flat on his bicycle, or something else may have happened. But, now our passports were stamped and legal to start our adventure home the next morning.

Before we would head back to the boat, food and supplies and much-needed bottles of rum were required. We visited a few of the local stores to load up. Now safely back, we got the *lady* ready for her visit at the fuel dock and tested the new reserve bladder fuel tank so we could make it home. Everything was looking good, so we headed back to our slip for some rest and relaxation. I met the owner of a Custom Motor Yacht docked nearby and was told he was the second richest man in the marina. I made the mistake of playing poker with him that evening. He's now the richest man in the marina!

Soon after my rapid monetary weight loss, Emanuel whipped up some of his specialty Nicaraguan-type meals as we settled into our evening movie since I had no money left to go anywhere. The movie for the night: *Mission Impossible- Rogue Nation* who would've guessed?

With a long journey ahead, I retired to my cabin for a nice shower and bed. The next morning, Cub was in his usual spot on the floor, and I stepped over him to turn off the TV set, being careful not to touch him or suffer the consequences. With everyone up and loaded with coffee, we untied about 7 a.m. and pointed the bow north towards San Andres, our first stop. This portion of our journey was about 200 nautical miles and the shortest run.

San Andrés is about 140 miles from the coast of Nicaragua and north-eastern Costa Rica, and 470 miles northwest of the coast of Colombia. I was surprised how San Andrés has a relatively flat topography and at its highest point in the island reported at an elevation of 180 feet above sea level.

We pulled in around 5 p.m. to the harbor's entrance and headed to a marina at the northern tip of San Andres for fuel and an overnight stay. If we could've cleared Customs, we would have fueled and left, but getting this done when we arrived was impossible. Before we docked, Cub asked me if I remembered how to do a Mediterranean moor?

Sure, I replied. What could go wrong just setting the anchor?

He orders me forward to the anchor winch and all he tells me is that I might have to give the anchor a little tug to get it moving. So, I undo the safety latch and wait for the command to "let go the anchor."

"Okay," he says, and I release the brake on the winch and nothing. So, I'm a-tugging, and the anchor drops just a little. I'm a-tugging, and he's a-yelling, and the anchor drops more and stops. I'm still a-tugging, and he's still a-yelling as he backs the boat towards the pier. Now he's yelling louder. Then Emanuel shows up to help. He opens the anchor hatch to find the chain all tangled up below. In he goes and soon the anchor falls. All this time Cub has been trying to hold the boat steady in 20-knot winds. Safely secured to the dock, we begin the fueling process again, and Cub talks with a few people to obtain some local knowledge.

While at San Andres, Emanuel hiked to town for some much-needed Subway sandwiches. The Port Captain was telling Cub to be on alert for an old steel trawler using distress signals to draw your attention, and once you approached to help, they would ram and try to stop your vessel. "If you don't see this boat on fire, I advise that you do not stop," he said.

With the fueling done, we settled in for some rum and food and to watch our evening movie. At the dinner table, I apologized to Cub for the anchor foul up, but he insisted he wasn't yelling.

"Cub, I take great pride in making you look good, just like I do when Shawn's docking the BARBARA LEE against an off-dock wind with the marina's tug boat back in Sanford." I always make him look good, except on the golf course!

It was a relaxing evening, and we watched – you guessed it – *Mission Impossible- Rogue Nation*. I was settling down and looking forward to an enjoyable long night's sleep and a day removed from Panama. Under different circumstances, like not carrying anything into their country, I would like to return. I just fell in love with the place, and the people I met during this trip were helpful and friendly. Bocas Del Toro reminded me of an old Key West back in the States, and well worth a return visit. It is a remarkable place to find yourself with its lush tropical vegetation everywhere you look. If you like diving and snorkeling, this is a great place to visit with an abundance of natural beauty. Bocas del Toro is not just a beautiful area blessed by nature but is an example of coexistence and multi-cultural respect for everyone.

CHAPTER 15

San Andres, Colombia

San Andres, Colombia to Roatan, Honduras
Departed Thursday at 0700 – Arrived Friday, February at 1600

The morning came early as I stepped over Cub, sleeping on the floor, to turn off the TV set to our favorite movie *Mission Impossible- Rogue Nation*. With everyone up and coffee made, we readied our *lady* for sea. I was finally back in the groove and getting accustomed to handling larger lines and fenders and our troublesome anchor winch. It was my responsibility to secure all lines and fenders and make sure all decks were cleared for sea. To check and ensure the safety straps on the center console stored on the retractable swim platform were secured without tripping over our coffee storage tank, cleverly disguised as a bladder fuel tank. To duct tape the engine and thruster control box cover on the aft deck where Cub maneuvered the vessel while docking and to make sure the rum was protected from the powerful movement in heavy seas. And, finally, the DVD of *Mission Impossible- Rogue Nation* had to be safely secured in our abundant movie library. I was also reminded not to forget to retract the big screen TV inside the cabinet.

With the boat untied and the anchor and chain safely aboard, washed and locked, we departed with a favorable weather report, which is always a good start. We made our way around this island to the north. Seas were 4 to 6 feet with the northwest winds of about 20 – 25 knots. We set north by northwest heading and propelled her cruising speed to about 10 knots. We were about 40 miles off the coast and approaching Eastern Honduras at sunset when Emanuel came below to wake me.

"Luke, Captain wants to see you topside for an extra pair of eyes."

Have you ever had that moment when you wished you were somewhere else? Like in the last chapter where I wanted to be somewhere else, or perhaps back one more chapter when I haven't landed yet in Panama, and I'm still asleep in my own bed? (My daughter is going to just love this!)

It was a Thursday evening when we spotted 4 skiffs in pairs about a mile off, and we were heading right for them. Trying to figure out their intentions with the binoculars in rough seas became another mission impossible, and in the cold breeze and darkening skies, I started to sweat because I wasn't getting a comfortable feeling. I noticed four individuals in one of the skiffs. As Cub altered our course to almost 45-degrees to port the one group was now on our starboard beam; the others were probably reading my book with interest in our easy stern access I mention later in the chapter. We decided that we were not waiting around to see if they were pirates or fisherman in a hurry, heading the same direction we were. Since we had no weapons aboard, all we had were size, speed, two guys from Sanford, and our trusted Nicaraguan friend Emanuel.

It sure looked like an ambush, so we throttled up, and they kept up. That's when fear had just about taken over my entire body. Do you remember when your high school teacher said math would come in handy one day? They were right! For example:

[X] = fuel consumed per hour by figuring in -
[Y] = 629 gallons of fuel we had left. Then, you divide misery by -
[D] = 220 nautical miles to go while cruising at -
[S] = 20-knots with the help from -
[C] = 1.5-knot current but heading into -
[W] = 25-knot winds while being chased by a fast moving -
[PIE] = Pirates in Equation. Your final exam question: How screwed are you by consuming 108 gallons per hour?

AND, what would happen if we lost our GPS tracking system during this terrifying engagement and we had to rely on my Celestial Navigation Training skills? This brought back my recurring nightmares of needing to pass my one question final exam:

You're in the Azores, south of Flores Island. 5 April 1985, about

0510, morning twilight, observed planet Jupiter. Hs 19 degrees 36.5 minutes at W.T. 5h 08m 14s, W.E. on Z.T. 30s fast, I.C. – 2'0, Ht eye 20 feet. Solve for Line of Position (LOP) - Yes, the actual question and my lucky guess correct answer of - 39 degrees North, 31 degrees 13 minutes west. See I did pay attention in someone's class. I still have my answer sheet for that test I took over thirty years ago. I had very few eraser marks and no blood stains like my typical chart plotting work. I usually stab myself with the navigation dividers or catch my fingers in the parallel ruler!

This, our longest run of just over 400 nautical miles (460 car miles), should take us about 34 hours if we finally get lucky. We couldn't keep this speed up, as it was consuming our precious fuel reserves. This boat doesn't run on coffee although we had a ton on the back deck inside a cleverly disguised bladder fuel tank. As the skiffs faded into darkness, we shifted into plan whatever-it-was-called and went into Stealth Mode, accomplished with all lights out, taped or smashed; even the little light on the refrigerator was turned off. So, we watched, and we listened, and I even went to the galley to grab knives. I taped the knives to my body and quickly transformed myself into the Duct Tape Ninja. I was now the ultimate fighting warrior and the guardian of our vessel and her crew. Nothing was getting past me tonight. I was It! The last defense, the illusionary protector of life and property!

When I felt I was in control, Cub came down off the bridge and said: "What the hell are you doing?" And "Did I not tell you not to leave your Tootsie Roll Pops lying around. Just look at this mess!"

"Sorry Cub!"

Needless to say, it was a restless night for all. I slept on the wet and windy—cold— bridge with the emergency beacon. I can joke about it now and look forward to what tomorrow may bring, but Cub had to trim about 50 miles off our route because of our diminishing fuel supplies. This course adjustment put us very, close to the Honduras mainland. How close you ask? Too damn close!

Let's recap this memorable run: We're a rather large moving target with no running lights and a stone's throw away from the mainland of Honduras! How about we get a little closer so outlaws, crooks, robbers, thieves, thugs or gangsters need not travel far, especially in bad weather, to reach us! Or, maybe the Honduras Coast Guard thought we were just a lost bunch of old guys out on a night cruise who forgot to turn our running lights on?

So, Kid, the next time I say, "Let's go to a place like Bolivia," let's go to a place like Bolivia! Well, they didn't film the movie in Bolivia, but in the direction we're running to – Mexico, pretending they were in Bolivia while I was pretending I was somewhere else!? I know some of you didn't get that reference. It's from the movie, *Butch Cassidy and the Sundance Kid*, starring Paul Newman and Robert Redford, released in 1969, just before I graduated from high school in Pennsylvania. My teachers were probably relieved that I left the area. Yes, that's how that night went, except I didn't *sleep* with the emergency beacon; I did *hang out* with it all night.

When we entered this area, we were surprised to see these 4 skiffs in rough seas so far offshore. Now, whether they were pirates, smugglers, fishermen or Barometer Bob, wanting to sell us a new movie DVD is anyone's guess. I would've felt better if we were armed. We had picked up this vessel in Colombia, which explains why we had no weapons aboard. But, we had Captain Cool, and I've seen him drop kick a few guys (for not attending to the protocol for waking him) without breaking a sweat. AND, we had Emanuel, who never left the bridge, and has the eyesight of a peregrine falcon.

I was always asking him: "Do you see anything? What about there? How about over there? And there? How about over my left shoulder? Check my right?"

AND then there's me - a chicken with his head cut off, packed with knives and looking for anything else I could use as a weapon—and hiding places. I needed someone like MacGyver aboard: hand him a blender, a straw, and duct tape, and he builds a tank. Perhaps, a canon for a boat.

Throughout the night, we all kept a watchful eye, particularly in the stern, since that would be the area of least resistance. The stern has a rather large extended small-boat platform for the vessel's 19' center console launch. The steps leading up to the main deck make it an easy access and any boarder's landing area of choice.

CHAPTER 16
Weather Delay – Roatan, Honduras

Arrived Friday at 1630

We approached Roatan an island located about 40 miles off the northern coast of Honduras. It is between the islands of Útila and Guanaja and is the largest of the Bay Islands of Honduras. I looked over the charts, and it seemed Roatan was just shy of 50 miles long and a little less than 5 miles at its widest point. We arrived on a Friday afternoon with high winds and heavy seas. We were glad we made it safely to this well-protected island, especially after last night's sightseeing tour and my self-anxiety arousal: aka Scaredy-Cat experience. I would have rather been at Disney's Pirates of the Caribbean adventure ride.

We passed through Brick Bay and made our way to the marina near the town of Los Fuertes, about 5-miles northeast of the Port of Roatan cruise terminals. The marina's dockmaster, appropriately named "Angel," met our arrival: a fitting—reassuring—end to our adventure.

We secured our vessel to her slip and gave her a good scrubbing with fresh water. When we finished, our proud *lady* quietly rocked in the gentle breeze. The dock was well positioned, neat and organized and all within 50 yards of the pool, restaurant, and bar. The marina was even on its own little island. Alongside the boat slip was a beautiful walkway that led to a dock that jutted out into the bay. And at the end of the pier was a protected shelter with hammocks and a wonderfully relaxing view.

That evening, we tried the restaurant and were pleasantly surprised how good the food was, including a great meal selection and a full bar.

Angel, the dockmaster, was our waiter and the bartender as well! We were finally safe and even joked about our latest sea adventure and other things grown men who drink way past their prime do, like visit the bathroom way too often.

Now we're hanging out in Barefoot Cay until we get our next good weather window—hopefully, Monday. We hooked up with a local driver, named "Dakota" from San Francisco, Honduras, and spent the afternoon with him. He took us to Coxen Hole for some much-needed supplies. I just loved the ride, the company, and beautiful scenery. We stopped at a rather large grocery store and found everyone to be friendly, even the Canadians. Dakota, who was wearing a Pittsburgh Steelers sweatshirt, took pleasure assisting area tourists, especially those from Sanford. While continuing his tour of this charming and picturesque town, Dakota drove us around the shopping areas for additional items. A little later, we found ourselves back at the boat where Emanuel prepared another one of his specialty meals as we settled in for our evening movie, *Mission Impossible- Rogue Nation,* now one of my favorite movies. My gold digging in the sofas paid off with enough coins to play poker. I soon had the money back that I had lost to the rich guy. You see, Emanuel never played much poker, and every time Cub would raise just after I raised, it was always a bluff.

I woke the next morning again to find Cub at his regular place on the floor. I was just stepping over him to turn off the TV when one of my Tootsie Roll Pops fell from my pocket and was heading right for his body. I quickly turned around and dropped to my knees, like the fast-moving ninja that I am, and caught the candy just in time. It was like watching Ethan Hunt, in his first *Mission Impossible* movie, when a single drop of sweat streaking across the lens of his glasses is about to fall and trigger an alarm, but Ethan catches it just in time. Our Cub alarm, however, has a slightly different kick to it.

All day Sunday we organized and cleaned, and I took more pictures to show my Facebook family when I get home. I was looking forward to watching the Super Bowl at a local sports bar and unwinding a bit. So, with everyone ready, we made our way to the marina office. While waiting for our ride, we chatted with the security officer who is also a religious rapper. In his shirt pocket, he kept a small notebook journal where, throughout his day, he would jot down the messages he received from guests or his own spiritual thoughts.

Dakota soon arrived. He recommended a local hangout and said he would even join the group. So, we headed for Herby's Sports Bar and Grill at the Clarion Suites at Pineapple Resort just off the French Harbor. Great food and atmosphere that went along with watching an exciting Super Bowl, even though we were the only table cheering for Carolina! They sure love American football in Roatan. Or, maybe the visitors from the U.S. sure love their football while on vacation in Roatan.

I remember having to take care of the crew that night and getting them home safely since I was the only responsible and sober member of the bunch. You know, I don't remember getting back to the boat that night. So, thanks, Dakota!

With everyone finally in bed asleep, our possessed vessel turned on the radio to the outside speakers. Around 4 a.m., I heard someone pounding on the boat and a woman screaming; "You left the radio on!" Did I mention the screaming and that I can't even explain some of the other supernatural feelings I was having while aboard this vessel? This will be covered in my next book, *The Days of Wine and too Much Rum*.

The next morning, I was hoping that I wouldn't see or, God forbid, accidently run into this screaming woman, but with just the two boats at the dock, the odds weren't in my favor. Yep, sure enough, there they sat Monday morning as I stepped over Cub in his usual spot on the floor so I could turn off the TV. But before doing that, I wanted to watch one of my favorite scenes, the motorcycle chases in *Mission Impossible- Rogue Nation*. Then, stepping over Cub again, I made my way to the galley to make coffee for our awakening and fearless crew.

Before leaving the boat, I was preparing myself on what to say. I walked slowly towards the couple sitting by the pristine pool deck, pretending I was on my phone, and even stopped and talked to my imaginary friend alongside the pool deck. I thought this might freak them out and they would leave. I would glance over occasionally to see if they were still sitting there and kind of get a feel for the mood they were in since I have transcendental powers (detailed in my book to be published three years from now, advance orders receive a 50% discount).

I suddenly find myself face to face with her, and I can't apologize enough as I wipe the tears from my eyes. I reassure her that we are planning to leave this morning so they will not have to go through another night like that again. I explain that you can turn this radio off and mute the speaker, but it just turns itself back on with the speakers a-blaring. A few days later, we dismantled the system, its wiring and all.

I found the woman and her husband to be most gracious, and I continued talking with them both. I told them about our night getting here and what we went through with the pirate scare and all. Sure enough, their boat had been attacked some time back in the same area we passed through, but their boat didn't have the speed to outrun them, so had to take evasive action for hours until the pirates gave up. Authorities told the couple that if the pirates had boarded, they would have taken everything they could find on board. There were no recent reports of anyone being physically harmed. That may not always be the case.

After the pleasant chat, I headed over to the marina and walked through the ship's store to browse and talk with some locals. I stopped to speak with the marina's security officer for the last time. Then I made my way back to the boat to help get our *lady* ready for her next sea adventure. After I had untied the lines, we headed over to the fuel dock about 345 smoots away to top off the tanks and clear Customs. We all thought we would depart and leave our troubles behind.

CHAPTER 17
Roatan, Honduras to Isla Mujeres, Mexico

Departed Monday at 1230 - Arrived Tuesday at 1500

We finally received a favorable weather window to leave Roatan on Monday and were just finishing fueling when Captain Cub received terrible news. The Mexican authorities will not permit Emanuel to enter their country without a visa, and if aboard, will not permit our vessel to enter Mexican waters without being subjected to a fine and or confinement. Oh, boy, there's that "confinement" expression I know so well.

Cub looked at me, and I looked at Cub. Since I carried all the knives and bragged that I was the legendary Duct Tape Ninja, a merciless non-asset liquidator. I would get the chance to use my knives on our friend Emanuel while Cub would then throw him overboard! (Well, you know that just didn't happen, but the scenario is being considered in the movie script, and I have a few friends I would like to see play Emanuel if a movie is made!)

We had to say goodbye to Emanuel, the Falcon and wished him our best as he made his way back to Nicaragua. A nice person with high moral values and, boy, can he cook! We do miss him though we keep in touch occasionally. Once he left the boat, Emanuel then had to take a ferry to Honduras and from there, a bus through Honduras to his home country of Nicaragua. He said he would stay there for a few days with some friends before making his way back to Bocas Del Tora where he would do some repair work for a marina back in Panama.

Now it's only the Sanford boys to go it alone. With all the documents now completed after sending for the Customs Agent to return to the boat to remove Emanuel's name from the crew's manifest, once again we had a Good-To-Go for departure and depart we did. The weather forecast of NW winds of 20 knots and seas 4 - 6 feet created for our vessel just a slightly bumpy ride. We cleared the island and changed our heading to the north by northwest towards Isla of Cozumel. Oh sure, I just loved our great and accurate weather forecasts during this whole trip! Have you ever heard the saying, "The Point of No Return"?

Well, we reached it at our dreaded "pirate sunset," and the weather turned for the worst: westerly winds of 35 knots. We could barely make headway and were getting pounded to death! It was so dark I couldn't see the end of my nose even if I crossed my eyes, and there was no telling which direction your body would head next! Just like my favorite ride at Disney when riding Expedition Everest at the Animal Kingdom and going backward in complete darkness. A short time later, you're now going forward, and you start to see the light just before you exit the mountain. I never saw that circle of light that night, but I explain the "Circle of Light" theory in one of my next books, *"The Gospel According to Luke."*

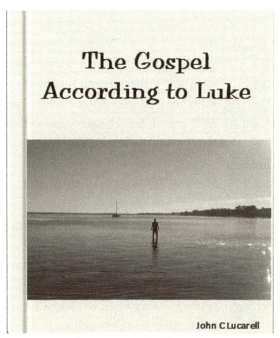

Photograph by: John Lucarell
The Gospel According to Luke

We anxiously looked over at the chart plotter for a good place to seek shelter, but a footnote at the bottom of the chart just said "Good Luck!" So here we go again, back to our normal pleasure-boating-turned-terror-cruise, and I was down to my least favorite Tootsie Roll Pop flavor. The only option was to change course from our more northern route to the west-southwest so the bow of the boat would be just off the headwinds to reach our closest protection, Bolivia. Sorry, I meant to say, "Belize," 60 miles to our southwest, and with that change in course, we were adding miles to this run. Our concerns mounted again about the fuel. I told Cub that maybe we should have put fuel instead of the coffee in that bladder tank!

All the safety equipment was set to go before our departure, and since only two of us were aboard for the remainder of our trip, we each carried a whistle. Cub wore it around his neck, but I had mine shoved elsewhere!

It's now around 3 a.m. and Cub tries to get sleep on a cushion next to the helm. He tells me, "If we start going backward, please let me know." Just then, the master alarm goes off, and the weather is so bad we can't get off the bridge to check; we must just hope for the best. A few hours later, Cub says, "Turn and keep the boat into the wind," so he can army crawl and go below and check the boat and the engine room. When he returns to the bridge, he says that everything looks good. Cub figures it might have been a stuck float switch on one of the bilge pumps forward, but there's no way he can reach that area in these high winds and pounding seas.

We had a search light at the bow, the best place to have a light because you get no bright reflections off the boat. But, you guessed it, ours pointed only straight up! I'm glad the light didn't work to see what was hammering us, or I'd be out of underwear! (Don't worry, Brandy, this is probably just a dream, go back to bed. Your dad is safe!)

A Post Planner's saying making its way through Facebook – "Life's journey is not to arrive at the grave safely in a well-preserved body, but rather to skid in sideways, totally worn out, shouting 'Holy Shit…. what a ride!'"

So, after a miserable night and Belize in sight, we get some much-needed protection from the mainland. Cub says: "Hug the coast and head north."

"How close?" I ask.

"Close enough without running aground!"

I went below later, and the boat looked like a mini battlefield. Things were everywhere, and we had to step over furniture, clothes, food, glass.... I found a chart book inside a shut cabin door and how it got there is still a mystery. And, oh look: A Tootsie Roll Pop!

With the change of course and our much-needed wind blockage from the mainland, we ran west of Banco Chinchorro, just off the coast of Mexico, and continued until we passed Cozumel to our east. If you ever get the chance to visit Cozumel, a must excursion would be to visit Rio Secreto. Discover this Mayan Underworld Cave Adventure at Playa Del Carmen on the mainland. Also, there are many gift shops throughout the picturesque town.

Well, we made it to Isla Mujeres, Mexico, with about 70 gallons left in our fuel tanks and with only about another 500 miles to go to make it back home to Fort Lauderdale. (I figured I could get about another two chapters from this trip if we forget to put on fuel while here in Mexico.)

CHAPTER 18

Weather Delay – Isla Mujeres, Mexico

We arrived safely at Isla Mujeres, Mexico Tuesday at 3 p.m. after leaving Roatan Monday around noon. Now waiting for a favorable weather window to head to Key West. "Weather Window," you hear that a lot when pleasure boating. I think it should be called *"whether or not* you get there on a scale of 0 to 5 based on the weather report." I will say this; this trip sure puts life in a different perspective. So, to help other travelers, I came up with this scale and call this forecast my Sea Tracking Endurance Prognostication Services (STEPS) which gives the boater a more detailed report and what to expect along the way. For example:

STEPS.0 – A good chance the weather statement you just received offers zero chance on making it to your next destination. If you decide to attempt departing at this time, concerned friends hope the Coast Guard shows up just in time as your boat sinks.

STEPS.1 – Much better odds than STEPS.0 but with seas approaching 10 feet you're scared and in doubt, and you run in circles, scream and shout just before you do an 180-degree turnabout. (poetry in real-time motion)

STEPS.2 – You make it but with a few bumps and bruises from 7 to 9-foot seas, but you're covered in salt, and you're in need of immediate medical attention from rapid weight loss from not being able to eat.

STEPS.3 – You make it through okay in 4 to 6-foot seas with just a few falls. Nothing funny to report.

STEPS.4 – You make it to your destination with seas of 1 to 3 feet but all along wishing for a smooth STEPS.5 forecast.

STEPS.5 – No such thing as STEPS.5.

We secure the 82 at the fuel dock at the northern tip of the island, and we wait, again, for Customs to clear us so we can go ashore. When you enter a country, the only person allowed to set foot on solid land is, and only, the Captain, but the documents and procedures vary from country to country when arriving. On arrival in Mexico, yachts must go to the nearest Port of Entry, with the Q and courtesy (yellow) flag flying.

Immigration must be cleared first. Then, the captain proceeds to Customs or, while at dockside with the ship's papers: the FMM forms (Multiple Migratory Form) and clearance papers. The TIP (Temporary Import Permit) is not part of the clearing in procedure and is obtained from Customs immediately after a vessel has cleared in. In reality, however, some Customs officials will not clear the boat into the country until the TIP paperwork has been processed. Sanitation (Health) is next, although this is not always requested. Finally, the Port Authority (API)—a fee based on tonnage is assessed by API at the first port of entry and must be paid at the port captain's office.

The Zarpe (an outbound clearance document, obtained from Customs and Immigration officials when you depart from a country you have been visiting) and ship's papers—six crew lists in Spanish—are required. Crew list forms (in Spanish) can be obtained either before or after arrival, on payment of a fee. All officials stamp and sign all crew lists, and each agent keeps a copy. For cruising in Mexican waters, a health permit is also required. Health officials may inspect the yacht, or the crew may have to visit the hospital for a health clearance.

Once you have cleared into the country, it is no longer necessary to clear in and out with the port captain at each subsequent port, provided you log in with a local marina and the marina keeps a record of arrivals and departures. See, Easy!

Now some have relaxed the rules and may allow the crews to go ashore nearby to eat, but I have encountered only a few who have offered that. This marina had a restaurant and bar you had to pass through when leaving the dock. I can only imagine, but few traveling boaters have ever made it thru to the other side. (That will also be covered in another book project, *The Final Minute.*)

My favorite part of waiting to clear Customs here in Mexico was the inspector that came aboard for food inspection. She came in, and we all did our pleasantries. She spoke English, and the conversation was going well until hunger pains took control of my body. Do you know when you take that first bite into an apple it makes that crisp biting sound? Yes, that sound as juices run down your happy face: kind of yummy sound?

It was at that moment she turns to the captain and asks, "Any fruits or vegetables aboard?"

Now I can't remember if an apple is a fruit or a vegetable but how am I going to explain this was only one of those decorative plastic apples, and it only looked real because I was so hungry! "You can eat only so many Tootsie Roll Pops. And I was fresh out," I whined! So, Cub replied that he was getting ready to go through the refrigerator and remove all that we had and dispose of them on shore.

The officer said, "I will take them with me when I leave."

She informed us we're okay with the other food stores aboard because we are considered a "yacht in transit." If we decided to stay for a longer period, all the food would be disposed of.

Can you imagine this inspector leaving with our bag thinking the fruit was from the USA, happy as hell skipping down the dock and she jumps and does that tapping both feet together, singing that happy American Beach Boys song "Vegetables"?

Well, I'm yelling back to her – "Enjoy the fruit, lady. It's from PANAMA!"

Isla Mujeres, Spanish for "Island of the Women," is an island in the Caribbean Sea, less than 4 miles off the Yucatán Peninsula coast across from Cancun. According to my charts, the island is less than 5 miles long and only half-mile at its widest part. The island is part of the Isla Mujeres Municipality in the State of Quintana Roo, Mexico.

We stayed for a few days, due to the weather forecast, so we enjoyed the island, especially the beautiful beaches just a few hundred yards away from the marina. The people were just an absolute pleasure! And you could walk and explore the town without that touristy hassle found at many Caribbean Islands when traveling on a cruise ship. The food was excellent and the drinks plentiful, and in the evening, the town came alive with Latin and American music and everyone having a great time. I would recommend staying on the island for at least a few days to explore the many stores and restaurants nestled is this picturesque island paradise.

I had visited the same bar the last time I was here—with Cub and Scooter over twenty years ago. It's still fresh in Scooter's memory and his mom's as he tells his side of the story. But, there are two shorelines to every ocean crossing, and this author went with his version!

CHAPTER 19

Next Stop Home—Mexico to the USA

Departed Thursday at 0730 - Arrived Friday at 1730

This is the final voyage of the small ship SUNSEEKER. Our mission to seek out Latin countries, foods I can't pronounce, strange and intimidating phraseologies (I finally used a big word) and to go where I haven't been in years. The doctor's office!

    This is my last chapter with a plan to make Key West as our entry into the U.S., clear Customs (hopefully) and head home to Palm Beach. This day we received our STEPS.2 forecast from the Sea Tracking Endurance Prognostication Services, and the next attempt would be in 5 days. It is a Thursday morning, and we must have been watching *Mission Impossible- Rogue Nation* again because the movie was still playing. Again, I had to step over Cub to turn off the TV set, but being careful not to touch or disturb him or suffer the consequences like in the other Chapters. But, by now I have developed a Wake-Up-The-Cub plan by placing his coffee within nose reach and then slowly backing away. Within minutes and to my amazement--his eyes open to a peaceful morning rise and no dreadful singing. With Cub now awake, we readied our *lady* and departed at 0730 from Mexico, hoping the Yucatan Straits offer forgiveness as reports for this area called for seas to reach 10-feet. Captain said anything more, and we must turn back to Mexico.

    I didn't mention this before, but all navigation was done on the exposed flybridge since the lower station navigation system was not working. Remember, the navigation system near the galley, the fully enclosed cabin with comfortable electrical adjustable chairs and with air conditioning, heat and all those unmarked switches! YES, that one! So here we go again! The winds increase and we must slow to 9 knots and be thankful it's still daylight. But, that dreadful pirate sunset is peering over our horizon! Before we get there, a wave picks us up and turns the boat in the opposite direction. I swear that even the autopilot screams, "What The Hell!"

Darkness arrives and, yes, and why not this problem of no running lights. We're entering the shipping lanes with nothing going for us but the searchlight that points straight up! So now we have to make a "call all night"—every hour on the VHF marine radio—with the international "calling" procedures such as the "Mayday" distress call, the "Pan-pan" urgency call, and "Sécurité" for navigational hazard call.

So here's my first radio call: "Sécurité - Sécurité - Sécurité – (This is the same guy from Chapter Five.) Now at position [so-and-so] with a heading of 060 degrees at 9 knots. Our running lights are inoperable, and we're using our bow searchlight and 2 candles (one held on top of the other at the stern) to alert vessels in our area. (thankful we had birthday candles aboard - the one's you can't blow out) This is SUNSEEKER standing by on Channels 13 and 16 for any concerned traffic." Concerned? They're probably laughing their butts off!

Later, Cub came up from doing an engine check, and I told him how I fixed the Searchlight: "You kick the control panel three times with your right foot, then hold the speed button down while pressing the Up or Down button."

"No way!" he says.

"I tried my left foot but couldn't get it to work, so use your right!"

Have you ever tried talking on the radio and you're freezing your butt off and making those funny shivering sounds as you speak? The other captains by now are worried that from listening to this all night, bad English might spread to everyone aboard! Okay, you got me! We didn't use candles; we ran with our stern floodlights. Oh, yes cold! I had two marine heavy weather type jackets, blanket, space heater, and a blow dryer for backup. Plus, the working hours were brutal! Two hours on watch and two hours off, continuously for 34 hours, and that was just for this run! I figured 10 more weight-loss cruises like this one, and I'd be down to my high school weight!

Hooray, daylight, and we're in the Gulf Stream just off of Cuba. However, you don't want to be here when the wind is out of the North and blowing 28 knots all day long. The Gulf Stream flows north, and I don't see another Italian out here. These colliding mammoths make for an un-pleasurable ride while your pleasure boating for the day. I told Cub that if he wanted to get out of this weather, we could head to Cuba, and I wouldn't mind if we surrendered to the sea!

Late afternoon, we have Key West in sight. But, with our usual luck, all three of Cub's phones do not work, and all his travel information and contacts are inside one of those little phones. He had one for International calling (for the boat's communications with the outside world); one of his own while in the States, and one for South America. Yes, not one works. We have only my personal phone, which is usually not in working and serviceable condition during this trip. So, trying to find dockage unannounced is a task, especially when most marinas are full. Finally, luck comes our way: we settle in at the beautiful Key West Resort and Marina with an actual working wifi system. You would think to find safe land with food and people who speak English, and candy stores would be an exciting accomplishment. No, it's wifi and your Facebook posts that matter most. AND, we arrived safely at a non-pirate sunset!

So, after fastening the 82 to the dock, we quickly washed her up to show our appreciation for a safe journey and our many amazing stories along the way. A call into Customs was a must, providing instructions to proceed to their office at the local airport in the morning. We now had plenty of time to have our smuggled 966 kilograms of coffee stored in our cleverly disguised bladder fuel tank unloaded under darkening skies. In the meantime, we could head to town for some food and drink.

Now with the 82 sitting legally in American waters and the alcohol wearing off, we settle in to enjoy our late-night movie. Trying this time to at least find a different film, I busily look through our abundant cinema selection: *Beneath...* - naaa too scary - *Deep Blue Sea* - naaa too not real - *Bermuda Triangle* - naaa I get lost following - *Open Water* - naaa been there - *Flipper?* - *Flipper* it is!

It is now Saturday morning, and Cub isn't in his normally-found position when I wake. I guess *Flipper* was just too much to endure last evening with not much alcohol. Why there he is in the galley! He's making …. Oh no – out of coffee! How can that be possible! So, instant coffee it is. Boy, what a joy!

A little later we find ourselves in a taxi, hopefully riding with someone who speaks English to my delight. Nope, the driver, is from Russia! Oh well, as we head to the airport to clear Customs.

What a pleasure to meet professional working-type people! Since the 82 is a foreign flagged vessel, more procedures are required, but the U.S. Customs Office is a sight for sore eyes. They soon have us on our way.

We finally departed Key West at 0945. With a favorable—STEPS.4—weather forecast, we kicked it into high gear and scooted at 20 knots (23 mph car speed) just off the coast and made Fort Lauderdale at 1830: yep, Pirate Sunset! We safely secured our *lady* to her dock—No running lights required.

THE END!

BUT….

The adventures will continue with another exciting book of sea life—semi-retired!

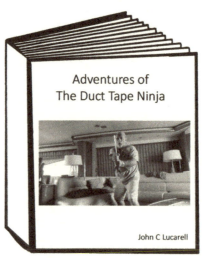

Picture by: John Lucarell
The Duct Tape Ninja

BUT WAIT – THERE'S MORE!

When you buy a copy of *The Adventures of the Duct Tape Ninja*, you'll receive an autographed copy of "*Juiced, My addiction to Ninja Kitchen Products,*" plus a month's subscription to Shipwrecked News

Picture by: The Cartoonist
Juiced, My Addiction to Ninja Kitchen Products

Your subscription to *Shipwrecked News will* keep you in tears as you read the latest in news, stories, and information for the Nauticool boater.

Photograph by: Heritage Old Time Portrait Studio
Shipwrecked News

JOHN "LUKE" LUCARELL

The Nauticool Dictionary

No definition in this Dictionary is to be regarded as affecting the validity of any trademark.

Vesseligamist - A person that owns more than one boat.

Boatlash - The sudden movement of one's own body, when the captain, pulling away from the dock, forgets to untie that last dock line.

Following Sea - Suggestive of paranoia; showing unreasonable distrust aboard ship.

Flying Bridge - the Unidentified flying object of an unknown nature. A few captains under the influence swear they have seen one of these.

Echo Piloting - A crude method of determining the depth of the water by throwing the first mate overboard and hearing him or her yell how deep it is.

Ketch - A fast moving two-masted fore-and-aft-rigged sailing vessel with a mizzenmast stepped aft of a taller mainmast but forward of the rudder.

Schooner - A faster-moving sailing vessel with two or more masts—all are fore-and-aft-rigged.

Yawl - A slow-moving sailing vessel, usually caught by a ketch but sooner by a schooner.

Bedding Compound – A sleeping berth holding more than one person.

Boom Vang - An audible discharge of intestinal gas.

Dead Reckoning - The estimated drift of a Boom Vang.

There is literally no end to the list of boating terms found in the Nauticool Dictionary, and I know you'd like to own one soon. Stay tuned for an exciting offer that will change your ways and make you a better boater. As you gain experience in this form of recreation, your vocabulary will broaden proportionately and naturally. It is hoped, however, that your enthusiasm for boating will not cause you to toss indiscriminate *Avast*, *Ahoy*, and *Belay*s into every conceivable nook and corner of your conversation. Also, strained efforts to force a thunderous Boom Vang are conspicuously inappropriate.

How to Fight Boat Sickness

If you're a queasy boater, there are alternative anti-sickness options may help settle your stomach. Captain Luke, M.D. (Monroe Dockmaster) who wrote *Traveling on a Bum Knee*, suggests these 5 strategies to fight boat sickness:

1) If someone aboard is about to get sick, turn up the stereo which is an excellent way to block out the gagging, retching, gurgling sounds produced by the afflicted person.
2) Concentrate on a distant point such as Capella and listen to *Don't Cry for Me Argentina*. The star Capella can be seen most nights at 31 degrees 50 minutes and its azimuth is 316 degrees. Of trifling interest is the meaning of its Latin name.... *little she-goat*.
3) Hang onto your equilibrium by avoiding aspirin, tranquilizers, alcohol, back flips and aerobic workout tapes.
4) Induce vomiting by staying on deck and reading Shipwrecked News, Volume 51.
5) Try applying pressure to the armpit without making that funny quacking Boom Vang sound.

Ask Huggablebaldy

If you have a question? - <u>He has the answer!</u>

Photograph by: John Lucarell
Huggablebaldy

Dear Huggablebaldy - I have a stern drive boat kept in the water on Lake Monroe. How often should I inspect my outdrive for corrosion and what is wrong with your eyes? Signed: *James T. Anode*

Dear Mr. Anode - Since your aluminum outdrive is accessible to galvanic corrosion, creature eaters, and unknown water things, I recommend a haulout and inspection every 4-6 months. In technical terms, Lake Monroe registers 1050 millivolts with a positive accelerator. Your outdrive contains 83% ASTM B418 iodinestic metal with a deterioration factor producing a negative compounded charge of 3% shielding at 350 milliamperes with a corrosion factor of 3.28 on the COR_1984 Monitor Scale. This accounts for corrosion in a brackish environment. As for my eyes, this is a direct corollary of rheumatoid arthritis of the Rhinencephalon, which is the olfactory region of the brain, in the cerebrum. This causes nitrogen-fixing bacteria of the genus that forms nodules on my optic nerve causing an unnatural look.

Dear Huggablebaldy - I purchased a new boat and was wondering if it was a good idea to buy a marine VHF radio? Signed: *Lester*

Dear Lester - A VHF radio would be a sound investment and necessary should a problem arise while out on the water. Picture this - You're cruising along when one of your passengers becomes nauseated from reading *Nauticool Hand Luke's Shipwrecked News*. You know you must contact an English teacher immediately, but you're without a radio. It may be hours before help arrives and by now bad grammar has spread to everyone aboard. Don't take the chance! Invest in a good marine radio.

Dear Huggablebaldy - I have been using my boat in the evening, and as soon as the sun goes down, I get attacked by those nasty blind mosquitos. What can I do? Signed: *Marie Culicidae*

Dear Ms. Culicidae – The next time you venture out in the lake at night during blind mosquito season get MAD (Monroe After Dark) or just get MADDER (Monroe After Dark Deterrent Evening Rinse). Just spray it on and forget it. No more scrubbing or rinsing those nasty midges from your hair. It's also ideal for minor scratches or as a bacteria-fighting mouthwash.

Dear Huggablebaldy – I'm a new Lake Monroe dockage customer and have been diagnosed with Invoice Congestion. How serious is this and how successful is the marina's Rehab Center? Signed: *Christie Credit*.

Dear Ms. Credit – Your condition is not a big deal at all. With plenty of sleep and watching what you spend at the marina, your problem should clear up in no time. In the first month, the Lake Monroe Rehab Center treated 52 cases. The most common ailment was Diadebit. Caseworkers have found that a person with Diadebit often drifts into a state of Credit Unbalance. Lake Monroe Researchers have linked people with symptoms of a credit unbalance when reading Shipwrecked News and their marina statement within the same hour. Rehab Director Lutz Lupesco made recommendations to the marina office staff to mail Shipwrecked News and their marina statements separately.

Announcement

Lake Monroe Marina is taking applications for their boating course in regulatory buoys. This free course alerts the boater and protects the manatee. They now offer a quiz you can take in the comfort of your own home. We encourage you to take this test before leaving the dock. We hope you become more aware of the regulatory zones you will encounter and the specific regulations of each.

Instructions: Circle the correct answer on the two definitions below. No eraser marks!

Manatee Zone – Slow Speed

   A) An area where boats must be off plane, settled into the water and proceeding without a wake or with minimal wake.
   B) A reminder it will take another day to reach Hontoon State Park 17 miles away.

Manatee Zone – A Much Slower Speed

   A) An area frequently inhabited by manatees, therefore requiring caution by boaters to avoid disturbing or injuring the manatee.
   B) An area frequently inhabited by biologists, requiring caution by manatees to avoid ganging up so as not to be miscounted.

If you answered B-B (and laughed), you shouldn't have. It will seem like it will take an extra day to get to Hontoon State Park.

If you answered A-A, give yourself 100 points. (Go Manatees!)

If you answered A-B or B-A, results are not in. Check back later in our next issue.

Shopping Ideas—Adopt a Florida Boater

Those looking for a unique, thoughtful gift can now adopt a Florida Boater for someone you love. The Lake Monroe Area Florida Boater made the endangered species list with implementing restricted speed limits and higher fuel prices.

For only $20, Save the Lake Monroe Area Florida Boater Club will send an adoption certificate, a photo of the adopted boater and a one-year subscription to *Sinking Fast*, the Lake Monroe Area Florida Boater Newsletter. For those who collect boating mementos, the club features an array of items in its new gift catalog, including the album **MAD**, *Monroe After Dark,* which features such hit songs as Mister Sandbar, Midge River, and Hitting the Dock in the Lake. Parents can get a year's worth of enjoyment as they read updates about their adoptee in each issue of the club's newsletter. Adopting a Boater is a great gift idea suitable for anyone and is an exciting way to learn about boaters and their environment.

In general, any single adult or married couple is eligible to adopt. A person may not adopt a Lake Monroe Area Florida Boater who is his or her wife, husband, brother, sister, uncle, or aunt or has a larger boat than you do.

Lake Monroe Fishing Report

Recent reports of fish being seen in Lake Monroe have been verified by Lake Monroe's very own, Embry-Riddle Aeronautical University Grad, Uncle Dave, aka Louie Fishsticks. On a recent flyby, Dave swears he saw at least ten Speckled Perch. However, an eyewitness claims the plane popped one in the head while landing thus reducing the fish count to nine. As this report filtered through Sanford, hundreds of fishermen are expected to try their luck at landing the seaplane. For updates on the Lake Monroe Fish Report or the latest in our new fly-fishing techniques, you can always trust the Pros of Monroe!

Around Town

The 5th Annual Lake Monroe Marina's Cattle Drive & Slumber Party was held at Brian's 100 acres ranch last week. This authentic working cattle spread ranch was fun for those who took their horseback riding seriously. Guests rode under the watchful eye of big game and experienced the wilderness solitude of Brian's backyard. For the rafting enthusiasts, Brian's river basin boasted the finest selection of whitewater runs in the state and only minutes away from wildflower hikes, fly fishing, bike trips, and jeep tours.

"I was at Brian's house and discovered an ancient Indian site, dinosaur bones, and an unusual geological formation right next to his house. Florida's best kept secret!" *Cheryl D, Deltona.*

Nauticool Boat Personals

Attractive & Single – 35-footer desires long-term commitment. Must enjoy anchored nights and outdoors. Dynamic personality looking for a non-smoker. A Fuming Gasaholic! BoatAd 3382

Adventurous Lady – Tired of sandbars and rainy days? I'm a stunning 30-footer with an enclosed cabin and loaded with features. BoatAd 6712

Gorgeous Gal – 40-year-old with beautiful lines, healthy with a touch of class. I love having my bottom maintained by someone who knows what he's doing. BoatAd 9023

The Laughter Chatter

After working all these years at the marina, you get the opportunity of witnessing some amazing things. Take the following conversation regarding our wifi system. I thought I'd heard everything! I received a call from someone having trouble connecting to our wifi, and I figured since we're always having trouble with our wifi, (and I get to use more of my run-on-sentencing techniques) I thought this must be a legitimate problem. [phone rings]

{Marina} Thank you for calling Monroe Harbour Marina. May I help you?
{Boater} I can't seem to connect to your wifi.
{Marina} Sir, what dock are you on?
{Boater} I'm in Sierra Bravo.
{Marina} Where?
{Boater} In your southern basin on a mooring.
{Marina} Sir, we have no southern basin, just east, and west with docks.
{Boater} Well, I see no docks just moorings.
{Marina} Sir, are you at Monroe Harbor in Chicago by chance?
{Boater} Yes!
{Marina} Sir, we're in Florida and our wifi signal fizzles out at 300 feet!
{Boater} CLICK!!

Provolone, by Roth Raclette

500 years ago, Christopher Columbus sailed into the unknown. His four ships, later known as "Quatro Cinco" The Nina, Pinta, Little Luke, and the Santa Marie, carried the intrepid sailors through storms and starvation to what was to become the New World. Local historians discovered documents dating to 1502 when Columbus stayed at his summer home in Osteen. Chris often traveled to the peaceful surroundings of Sanford to visit local merchants and occasionally buy a few items. For safe keeping, Chris would place them in his secret chest.

"You can never have enough front-end alignment coupons with the roads the way they are," replied Chris. His car, a 1497 Pinta XL Sedan, named after one of his ships, was out of warranty and always in the shop.

Then the nightmare began. Christopher's estranged wife, Ricotta Figaro had stolen his secret chest. It was a rainy day that July 31, 1502, when a crew member started up the 16hp diesel and moved the tiny ship, "Mozzarella," over to the fuel dock before the marina closed. The vessel was loaded and with everyone aboard they headed towards the haunted island of Muenster near Butchers Bend at the treacherous waters of the "Big Whirl." Ricotta knew they would be safe there because no one would venture near this island, not even Chris. As night fell, the crew sang and danced around the campfire.

They were all there – Ailsa Craig, Lacy Swiss, Anejo Enchilado, Sage Derby, Feta Parmesan, and Ricotta. They were all at ease and drinking plenty of BUD BROWN, a popular Lake Monroe beverage.

Then suddenly, "Feta" yelled out - "PROVOLONIES," a band of tourists from Palatka!

Later captured and delirious from drinking too much Bud Brown, Ricotta would scream out for no reason. The worried Provolonies were afraid this crazy woman would release Rattus, the local cheese eater and evil spirit of the Provolonies. Fearful, Cheddar Carlow, the tribal leader, sought help from Alma Vorarlberger, the Provolonies' tour guide. Some 200 years earlier, Rattus had been evicted from his home on this island for making faces at passing Provolonies. Before Ricotta was captured, she buried the chest.

To this day, the hidden chest has not been recovered. Immediately after the capture, the seized vessel, "Mozzarella," was put up for sale. Alma called his friend, Ted Gorgonzola, editor of the "Gouda News," and placed this ad in his newspaper:

> **Old but Unique** – Not much action for this 52-footer, but I can still keep it up – sank only once. Looking for a *lady* with a sense of humor. BoatAd 3288

The "Mozzarella" was sold a short time after to Abbaye de Belloc. She kept the boat in Sanford for about a year until finally moving the vessel to be near her boyfriend, Prosciutto, in Sandwich, Massachusetts.

How I Spent My Summer Vacation by Peegori

There is always something said about the open road. Onward and upward to that great State of Pennsylvania. I was making this trip to seek old friends, family, and, with some luck, smooth roads through the state. To boldly go where I hadn't been in years—the alignment shop! On my visit, I learned that some of my old friends had passed away, and my family had moved. Bummer vacation! I should have called.

On my return to Florida, I stopped off to do a little calm water rafting, made famous by the movie "Throw Away the Anchor." The Twin Nostril on the upper St. Johns River has a mild but intimidating character. I paddled through streams lined with trees and stumps with colorful names like Broken Nose, Bloody Nose, and Snot-Nose. I even took a trip down the famed Ugh Nasal. Locals call the Ugh Nasal, The Rio de Las Pharyngeal, "River of the Runny Nose," where the river runs past areas where the Pollen counts tend to be highest. For me, this was the ultimate calm water challenge.

If you would like to take this trip, bring plenty of cash, reading glasses, and tissues because when you run the slow-flowing Ugh Nasal, you'll have plenty of time to read Peegori's Theory on Modern Marine Plumbing but they don't take credit cards! Allergies, it's everywhere you want to be!

Doggie Dodger by Buster

I remember several made up stories ago, back in Sanford: another dogfight, but with a dogmatist boater named David "Doggie" Dodger. Mister Dodger, who quickly pointed out to me the dog stuff littered along the walkway just past the dogleg on Pier B.

"Dog Poop!" yelled Dodger, with his voice becoming more dogmatized. Again, "What are you going to do about this increasing problem on these docks?" I quickly summoned someone to have the dock hosed off.

"How's that Doggie, referring to his nickname? Any better now?" I asked, pointing to the clean dock. He replied that his dog died yesterday and to not interfere with his personal life. I soon found myself engaged in a dogfight, just like in Panama. Soon after, he threw me into the water. Gasping for air and remembering I'm not in the Caribbean, swimming about in beautiful, clean blue water, but in the beautiful slightly tinted not-so-clear brown water where they make Bud Brown, the popular Lake Monroe Beverage of the St. Johns River. I attempted to dog paddle to safety, and I tried to get the attention of a nearby boater who was dognapping aboard his vessel Doghouse. Dog-tired, I finally made it back to the dock where I pulled myself to safety and right into a pile of – you guessed it!

In our next Issue of Shipwrecked News, let your dreams set the course. Also, the shocking report on how I was visited by an Alien on my birthday. Keep informed with *Notice to Navigation* and kick back with cooking tips from *Chef Harry*.

Special Thanks

I want to acknowledge all my friends who have helped share their lives through my voyages. It was my intent to make some of my readers laugh and maybe for a moment forget about the troubles we face in our day-to-day lives. To my publisher who tried desperately to keep me from using an extra particle in my subjunctive moods; to my loving daughter, Brandy, for her never-ending sleepless and horrified nights worrying about her father; for Lynn telling my daughter not to worry about her father; for Bud for having to listen as I told my stories time and time again; and to Shawn who is indeed an exceptional golfer for it was I trying to beat him. (Yes, that was my longest run-on sentence!)

I have reached my next destination, which has required my most extended voyage—Retirement! I can only hope to improve my writing and search for new adventures along the way. I planned to cover the expenses through my book royalties that many of my Meadville classmates and my twelve friends promised to buy!

Ultimately, I wanted to surround myself with...

Oh No, how can this be? Absolute Silence?! YES, it was too damn quiet at home! I needed the fast-paced action like being chased by someone or something when yachting with Cubby! I even caught myself peeking out my windows to see if I had any living neighbors. I didn't even hear a car drive by!

AND, then it happened, the author switched genres—from drama to mystery. It was early one morning when I heard something. That sound! That gasping-for-air kind of sound! I was alone, so it wasn't me this time.

The mystery now shifts to action and adventure. It was my lawn sprinklers! Yes, those! I quickly dressed and ran out the front door to see if they all worked! Yes, what a pleasant sound they all made. Just look at all that water, the green grass, the noise! I was saved from the profundities of silence! (Sorry, I just had to get that last big word in! It probably doesn't go with the sentence but consider the source.)

AND, then it happens. Cub shows up just as someone's house alarm is going off. With every passing second, the alarm is getting louder! We look around to check and don't see any activity in the neighborhood! Why no activity? Maybe I don't have any living neighbors? Was the Duct Tape Ninja involved? The Plot Thickens when the author uses a metaphor within a metaphor! (Sorry, I wandered off again.)

Actually, nothing ever happens in this neighborhood. It was my house alarm that was going off, and Cubby was probably off somewhere in the Caribbean without me.

Retirement! Troubled Times Await....

I will leave you with this thought – 28 degrees 51 minutes 25.60 seconds North, 81 degrees 21 minutes 14.02 minutes West.

Sorry, perhaps it was this thought - The passage of life takes us many places. Sometimes our limitations kick in. We fall. If we are strong, we catch ourselves. If we are less fortunate, we struggle. Through this journey, and with hope and perseverance, the path to life's precious treasures are within reach. Signed: Luke, b.1952.